Franc

ois Nepveu

The hidden life :

from Nepveu's Pense?es

Franc

ois Nepveu

The hidden life :
from Nepveu's Pense?es

ISBN/EAN: 9783741158148

Manufactured in Europe, USA, Canada, Australia, Japa

Cover: Foto ©Andreas Hilbeck / pixelio.de

Manufactured and distributed by brebook publishing software
(www.brebook.com)

Franc

ois Nepveu

The hidden life :

The Hidden Life,

FROM

NEPVEU'S PENSÉES.

DEDICATED,

BY PERMISSION,

TO THE REV.

H. P. Liddon, D.C.L.,
ETC., ETC.,

WITH DEEP RESPECT

FOR SINGLENESS OF PURPOSE,

AND A FAITHFUL USE

OF BRILLIANT GIFTS.

Translator's Preface.

THE following Extracts are translated from a popular French devotional work which has been rendered into every European tongue. Being thoroughly practical, and containing much matter in a small compass, they will probably be found a special help to meditation and self-examination.

May some readers, dissatisfied with that cold unloving propriety which characterises the easy religion of the day, and yearning after higher things, be led to a warmer love, and more zealous imitation of GOD their SAVIOUR.[1] May they realize in an increasing degree— taught perhaps of sorrow and bitter disap-

---

[1] Love is the mainspring of a devout life. In exact proportion to its strength, will it impel a man to the daily renewed sacrifice of his will and affections to GOD, and transform him into a faithful copy of CHRIST. This is the end of religion, and love alone can effect it.

pointment—that after all there are better
gifts and higher rooms of service than the
heaping up of riches, the winning of titles,
and self-seeking of every kind.

They need not wander far in search of
work. All are not called to uncommon labours. All need not exchange their homes
and their home duties for cholera wards and
fever-stricken dens of our great cities. We
need not despise little things, for they have
made great saints. The Gospel tells us of
Mary the Penitent washing her SAVIOUR'S
feet with tears and wiping them with the
hairs of her head, but of Mary the Blessed—
the holiest doubtless among women—not one
striking action is recorded.

Even they whose field of labour lies within
the narrowest limits—nailed perchance to a
sick bed—can give a good example, love, and
prayer. And what is more powerful for good
than these? "The best way to correct the
faults of others is to correct our own;" example is more winning than many words;
while love and prayer combined can move
heaven and earth.

Changes—social, political, and religious—are in store for England. Our future depends more, under GOD, upon the zealous co-operation of Clergy and Laity in every good work than upon the wisdom of legislators and the valour of armies. True religion is the backbone of a people. Let us then all do our part—some with ten talents, others with but one; let us love, and live for GOD, and He shall be *our help and our shield,*[1] and shall show us in His own good time and way "that lowly self-knowledge is more to be prized than the highest attainments of science, and that to mortify and conquer our own appetites in however trifling instances is more praiseworthy than to storm strong cities, to defeat mighty armies, work miracles, or raise the dead."[2]

M. J. B.

Conversion of S. Paul, 1871.

---

[1] Psalm xxxiii. 20.

[2] "The Spiritual Combat,"—S. Francis de Sales' favourite pocket companion, of which there is an excellent and cheap English translation.

Contents.

Contents.

THE HIDDEN LIFE.

The Mystery of the Epiphany.

NO sooner did the Magi see the Star in the East than they set out in search of JESUS. They had to leave their kingdom, and undertake a long and painful journey full of dangers and difficulties. They knew not whither they were being led, but they knew that it was to JESUS they were going. This thought was enough to make them surmount every obstacle, too happy if peradventure they might find Him. Alas! many a day has JESUS been calling me, and I have never answered; far from seeking Him Whom I know to be my GOD, I turn away; or, if for a time I seem to seek Him, the least difficulty is enough to discourage me.

To the faith of the Magi the stable and the manger appear a palace and a throne. The

lowliness, the poverty, the misery of the Holy
Child does not offend them. Their living
faith in that moment discerns the glory of
lowliness, the splendour of poverty, and the
true blessedness of seeming misery. They
recognise all the grandeur and majesty of a
GOD beneath that poor estate; His omnipo-
tence in that weak and helpless form; and,
transported with love, adore! But I, weak
and wayward Christian, am daily scandalised
by the humiliation and lowliness of my SA-
VIOUR. I, as well as they, have been taught
—aye, and convinced—by faith; I, too, recognise His Divinity; and yet—far from loving and adoring—my conduct proves how
much I despise and contemn that lowly
estate which He embraced out of love for
me!

The Magi were satisfied with no barren
niggard faith. Theirs was rich and fruitful;
they showed it in their actions. They offered to JESUS gold, and frankincense, and
myrrh, as visible pledges of the gift of their
hearts. To love, nothing appears too costly;
when the heart is once given, nothing is kept
back. And yet, alas! how long has JESUS
claimed my heart and I have never yielded
it; He has given Himself wholly unto me,
and I deem the price too great when in return

He would have me surrender myself wholly unto Him!

" The heart is not fixed, which is not fixed to the Cross."—*S. Aug.*[1]

𝔗𝔥𝔢 𝔑𝔢𝔢𝔡 𝔬𝔣 𝔕𝔢𝔭𝔢𝔫𝔱𝔞𝔫𝔠𝔢.

REPENT ye, and believe the Gospel,[2] saith the SAVIOUR. He places these two things together because the one is a necessary result of the other. It is impossible to believe in the truth of the Gospel without also believing in the necessity of repentance. No man can be saved without faith; no sinner can be saved without repentance. The faithful are indeed saved, but the faithful are all penitents. It is as impossible to enter the Kingdom of Heaven without the baptism of tears as without that of water. They are both equally necessary; the latter to efface original, the former actual sin.

Except ye repent, ye shall all likewise perish,[3] is another saying of CHRIST addressed to all sinners: and where is the Christian who is not a sinner? He excepts none, 'Ye shall

---

[1] The mottoes are mostly translated from the Latin.
[2] S. Mark i. 15.   [3] S. Luke xiii. 3.

all perish.' This threat concerns every one. Every sinner must repent in this world or the next. The damned repent in hell with *weeping and gnashing of teeth.*[1] Theirs is a cruel penitence as ceaseless as it is unavailing. They repent there of not repenting here. Surely the awful contemplation of the endless remorse of the damned should soften the harsh and forbidding aspect of timely repentance here; surely the severest discipline is welcome if it be a sure means of escaping eternal punishment.

O my SAVIOUR, Thou didst drain a cup of bitterness not Thine own in order to inspire me with courage, by Thine example, to taste it in my turn; I needed so powerful an example to draw me out of my apathy, and I still need Thy grace to support my weak efforts against self; without Thy help I am undone. Thou knowest that no man can hate his own flesh unless it be given him from above; he alone who is touched with Thy love can conceive this holy hatred; vouchsafe me such a penitential love as shall make me hate myself.

"According to the greatness of the sin must the repentance be."—*S. Ambr.*

---

[1] S. Matth. viii. 12.

Half-heartedness.

ALL sin must be renounced without exception. To retain one is to renounce none. You must *turn* unto the LORD, but it must be *with all your heart.*[1] To wish to divide the heart between GOD and sin is to rob Him of it altogether. In the Old Law there were divers kinds of sacrifices, but in the New, there are only holocausts, that is, sacrifices in which no remnant of the victim is reserved. Faith is a sacrifice of our reason; to disbelieve one article of the faith is to believe none. Confession is a sacrifice of our lips; consciously to keep back a single sin is not confession but sacrilege. Contrition is a sacrifice of our hearts; it must be a whole offering: if there is a single sin which you do not detest, this reservation renders your *sacrifice* not only of no avail, but *an abomination*[2] in GOD's sight.

Even among religious persons there are few who have not a besetting or darling sin which they indulge instead of mortifying. Some though upright are backbiters, others though pious are peevish and fretful; the sweet-tempered may be negligent and slothful; the in-

---

[1] Joel ii. 12.   [2] Prov. xv. 8.

dustrious but little weaned from this world's good things; the charitable and open-handed are perhaps self-indulgent, while the ascetic are more ready to take offence than to forgive. Other sins are willingly sacrificed to GOD, but the bosom-sin is kept concealed in the inmost folds of every heart. We imitate Saul whom GOD rejected because though willing to destroy that *which was vile and refuse*,[1] he spared Agag. His rejection was the penalty of misplaced pity; his crime lay in sparing one whom GOD had commanded him to sacrifice. And Christians are condemned for sparing some besetting sin, the sacrifice of which GOD has distinctly required. Often it is not the enormity or the number of sins which damns, but the fact that some one darling sin has never been sincerely confessed and laid aside. We act dishonestly towards GOD and ourselves by covering or palliating it, but alas! GOD is not mocked. It matters not what other sacrifices we make, so long as we spare the dominant sin, we arouse instead of appeasing GOD's displeasure.

"I had found the precious pearl, which, selling all that I had, I ought to have bought,[2] and I hesitated."—*S. Aug.*

---

[1] 1 Sam. xv. 9.   [2] S. Matth. xiii. 44.

Good Resolutions.

SORROW for past sins is not enough. There must be a sincere resolution never to commit them again. The test of sorrow for the past is the firmness of our resolutions for the future. We have reason to believe that we are truly penitent when we faithfully adhere to our resolution of sinning no more. The one is, as it were, a pledge of the other, so that when we fail to keep the one, we have every reason to question our good faith as regards the other. Past sins are not truly repented of when they are not henceforth avoided with constant firmness. He is an impostor and not a penitent, says S. Gregory, who finds pleasure in committing the very sins which he has, a moment before, bewailed.

Again, your resolution must be steadfast. Feeble purposings or good intentions are not enough : hell is paved with them. They can make men unhappy, but not penitent. To experience some distaste for evil, to be well-disposed, may amuse and deceive, but will not justify. It is not enough for a true penitent to say, I would. He must say, I will and I shall do it, cost me what it may. The former merely implies a conditional willingness which bears no fruit. "I would," means here, I would consent to give up this or that sin, were it not necessary at the same time to give up this or that pleasure or object. Willingness indeed! the term is self-contradictory. "I would," that is to say, GOD is urging me by His inspirations to forsake sin, and while resisting Him, I mistake the promptings of grace for those of my own liberty, bare sentiment for deliberate consent, and an inoperative desire of it for conversion itself. Is it not this which has flattered and beguiled you all this time; and which, by substituting a false and fanciful idea of repentance, has hindered you from ever repenting in earnest?

Once more, your resolution must be carried into effect. A man thinks he wills a thing when he forms a feeble desire. But, as he does not put his hand to the task and carries nothing out, he at bottom does not will it. He who really wills to give up a sin takes the proper measures, even the most painful and difficult; sets himself to overcome the greatest obstacles if they stand in the way of his good resolutions, and avoids all occasions of temptation, however agreeable to his interests and inclinations they may appear.

Is it after this fashion that you have willed to renounce sin? Then your good resolution was sincere and your penitence genuine. But if not, how can you rely on your confessions? Have you not need to repent of your very acts of repentance?

"God does not demand impossibilities; do what you can, pray for what you cannot do." —*S. Aug.*

Backsliding.

FREQUENT relapses cast a doubt on the genuineness of a man's repentance. He may rely on the sincerity of the confessions of his sins, and say that if he falls, he, at least, raises himself again through penitence. But the genuineness of that penitence is questionable which allows a man to fall again as soon as he has risen. Though the will be liable to change, it does not pass at once from one extreme to the other—from a sovereign loathing of sin, such as must ever be found in true penitence, to as strong a love of it, as is the case in deadly sin where the creature is preferred to the Creator. They are not implacable foes who are so soon and so easily reconciled. That is not a radical cure which admits of so speedy a relapse. No, frequent relapses look suspicious. They call in question the sincerity of the will. Can the will be sincere when it never carries out its intentions? When a man's will is self-conflicting one may say of it what one says of the will of GOD, that to will is to perform. Had you really willed to do what depended on yourself alone, you would have done it. Is it not your own fault if in spite of the help of never-failing grace you fall back into sin? You have promised not to do so, before GOD, a hundred times; you could have kept your word, for grace was vouchsafed you.

Frequent relapses leave your penitence open to doubt, because they make it uncertain whether you have received grace. The invariable result of genuine repentance is a fresh supply of grace which imparts great strength to resist the allurements of sin, and prudence to avoid those occasions which may lead to temptation. When we see, then, in the place of strength to resist sin a pitiful weakness in yielding, and instead of caution the same readiness to enter into temptation, we may reasonably assume that grace has not been received, and that your repentance has not been genuine.

"It is folly to purpose and not perform." —*S. Bern.*

The Desire of Revenge.

NOTHING is more natural than the desire of avenging an injury; and for this reason, nothing is more difficult than to forgive or love an enemy. And yet nothing is more necessary. None but a GOD could have given, none but a Christian can keep such a command. Being GOD, CHRIST says, *But I say unto you, Love your enemies.*[1] We give Him a convincing proof that we recognise His Divinity when we obey so difficult a precept. "But I say unto you," implies: I know that the world, that custom, that your prejudices, your passions, your reason forbid you, but *I* tell you the contrary. Which must you believe—which must you obey? It is I—your GOD, Who can command anything, and Whom you are bound to obey in everything—Who command this; I Who have reserved the prerogative of vengeance; Who will see you righted if you do not seek to right yourself; Who show no mercy except to those who show it to their brethren; Who have pardoned such grievous sins, and ask you in turn to pardon light ones. When

[1] S. Matth. v. 44.

I have forgiven *thee all that debt of ten thousand talents*,[1] oughtest thou to find it hard to forgive thy brother *an hundred pence*, when I animate thee by My example, strengthen thee with My grace, and hold out the alternative of eternal happiness or misery as thy reward?

Never is the authority which GOD, as the Fountain of Truth, exercises over man's spirit better shown than when it enables him through faith to triumph over his prejudices, and to believe that which appears inconceivable. Never is the empire of GOD, as the Principle of Law, so clearly exhibited as when it forces a man to resist his inclinations, and love that which is hateful,—the person of an enemy. GOD hath said it: you must believe though senses and reason say the contrary. GOD commands it: you must obey though heart and passion rebel. The subjection of the reason and the pardon of injuries are the truest homage and most acceptable sacrifice which man can offer to GOD as the Fountain of Truth and the Principle of Law. Without them no sacrifice can please Him.

"Human vengeance retaliates wrong for wrong, heavenly repays but love."—*Paulin.*

---

[1] S. Matth. xviii. 32.

The Advantages of Humility.

HUMILITY turns our very sins and vices to good account, while the want of it renders good works a source of danger and ruin. The publican was a great sinner, but he was humble: *He would not lift up so much as his eyes unto heaven,*[1] or approach the altar: he earned the praise of GOD! The Pharisee vaunted his virtues and enumerated his good works: pride made him fall: he was reproved! Thus humility makes sin the ground of righteousness, while good works become, through pride, matter for sin.

We should be grateful to GOD for having made salvation depend not on self-exaltation, but on self-abasement. Every one cannot exalt, but every one can abase himself. All cannot do great things, or form vast designs for GOD's glory; but there is not one who cannot humble himself. All have not the gift of prayer in an eminent degree; but who cannot humble himself in prayer, and thus achieve much while he seems to labour in vain? I cannot always do the good I would, but by always acquiescing in my inability, and

---

[1] S. Luke xviii. 13.

C

humbling myself before GOD on this account,
I can make good the defects of my actions.
I cannot be always praying, always fasting,
always sorrowing for sin, but I can always be
humble.   O humility, short but sure way of
attaining great sanctity at little cost !

" The Pharisee returns thanks for the sins
of others !"—*S. Bern.*

Profession and Practice.

MAN'S faith is GOD's glory. We honour
the Divine law by submitting our wills
to those dispensations which run counter to
our inclinations ; by loving that which the
natural man loves not, for instance, the person of an enemy. We honour the Divine
wisdom by yielding ourselves to His guidance,
even when He leads us by a way we have not
known, and in a direction opposed to our
tastes and interests. We honour the Divine
truth by believing that which cannot be tested
by the senses, nor conceived by the reason ;
which is even opposed to the experience of
the one, and the light of the other.
   Our faith reflects honour on ourselves while

honouring GOD. It exalts while abasing us; enlightens while blinding us; sets at liberty while taking us captive: for it delivers us from the thraldom of the senses. When I firmly believe the great truths of Revelation I participate in the infallibility of GOD; it is as impossible for me to err as it is for GOD. What strength, what elevation of mind, what glory, faith imparts! Oh, the weakness and wretchedness of those who will not seek its guidance!

Our faith honours GOD when our practice harmonises with it. To believe in a Being infinitely great, and yet not serve Him; infinitely good, and not love Him; infinitely righteous, and not fear Him; infinitely holy, and sin against Him,—is this consistent? To believe that *that which is highly esteemed among men is abomination in the sight of God*,[1] and yet hanker after this; believe that CHRIST has denounced woes against the rich and voluptuous, and eagerly desire to be such a one; believe that He blessed poverty and the tears of repentance, and fly from them in dread; believe that Heaven is reached through humility, and wish always to be exalted; that a Christian must crucify the flesh, and think only of pampering it; that the Kingdom of Heaven is

[1] S. Luke xvi. 15.

taken *by force,*[1] and spare oneself the least
hardness,—is this to act consistently?

Let us either change our faith or our practice. Not to believe these truths is infidelity;
to believe and not practise them is folly. *He
that believeth not,* saith the SAVIOUR, *is already
condemned.*[2] But he that believeth and liveth
as though he believeth not shall be still more
severely punished. If your faith be not the
rule of your daily life it shall condemn you.

"You are a sort of impostor when your
profession and practice disagree."—*S. Ambr.*

Grace abused.

NOTHING is more needful than grace,
and yet nothing is more abused. Nothing is more precious, and yet nothing is
more despised. The smallest measure of
grace is worth more than all the blessings and
pleasures of the world; the price paid for
grace was the precious Blood of our Redeemer. As often then as we abuse grace,
we trample under foot the Blood of CHRIST;

---

[1] S. Matth. xi. 12.   [2] S. John iii. 18.

and His death, far from being the instrument
of our salvation, becomes the aggravating
cause of our reprobation! When we become
insensible to the secret reproaches of conscience, when we stifle salutary remorse, close
our eyes to Divine illumination, and neglect
the urgent inspirations of GOD, do we reflect
that we are resisting, despising, and outraging
grace? Think we of the dangers and the
consequences of such a sinful course? Or
shall we begin to think of them when the evil
is past remedy? The damned in hell set its
full value upon grace, and shall eternally be-
wail their abuse of it. Eternally, but alas! in
vain shall they wish they could undo their
folly. The abuse of grace was the great
error of their lives; the remembrance and
deprivation of it shall form their everlasting
penalty. If you realized this would you resist those good motions which GOD is this
very hour vouchsafing? Alas! you thought
you had only your sins to dread, but the abuse
of grace is to be feared still more. Had you
received no grace, you had not been guilty,
and had you received less grace, you had
been less guilty. But, as it is, the poor
heathen shall be thy judge, weak and faithless
Christian, for if he had received but a small
portion of those graces which GOD has

lavished upon thee, perchance he might have become a saint. And since they have not made of thee even a Christian, they shall make thee a reprobate.

" Not grace alone, nor man alone, but grace working with man will save."—*S. Aug.*

The Loss of God.

THE most cruel penalty of the damned shall be the loss of GOD. The heart of man is an infinite void which GOD alone can wholly fill, but which, in this life, is taken up with a thousand distracting objects. Instinctively it feels drawn towards the Creator as its sovereign Good, but the manifold ties of the creature weigh it down and arrest its course. There is a natural perception of the beauty and grandeur of the Deity, but it is weakened and obscured by the burden of the flesh and the corruption of the senses. But as soon as the soul shall be separated from the body, and severed from all earthly attachments, it will realize this awful void. All that blinded it to the true knowledge of GOD shall be torn away ; the varied fascinations of the creature shall be no longer felt; GOD shall appear infinitely worthy of love and alone capable of giving sovereign felicity. But alas! an irresistible Arm shall be felt repelling all efforts to draw nigh, and a Voice heard saying, *Let him turn to his own house, and let him not see My face.*[1] Cut adrift from GOD the soul shall be tossed to and fro by the violence of conflicting emotions, incapable of loving Him whom it feels to be worthy of all love, and striving with unavailing efforts to reach its sovereign Good. Eternally drawn towards Him by an instinctive attraction, it shall be held fast under the dominion of sin, and impelled to hate Him Whom it is impotent to love. Eternally shall this sad thought prey upon the damned: I have lost my GOD for ever to gain a moment's pleasure, and in losing Him I have lost myself and everything besides!

" As the breath is the life of the body, so is GOD the life of the blessed. . . . . That soul cannot be said to live, which is alienated from the life of GOD."—*S. Aug.*

[1] 2 Sam. xiv. 24.

𝔖𝔞𝔩𝔳𝔞𝔱𝔦𝔬𝔫 𝔞 𝔭𝔢𝔯𝔰𝔬𝔫𝔞𝔩 𝔐𝔞𝔱𝔱𝔢𝔯.

OUR Salvation is our own affair. If we
fail, the loss is ours alone. No one
shall share it with us. In the business of
the world men are often content to share
their profits with others in order that these
may in turn share their losses. But in working out our salvation we must run all risks
alone. The whole profit or the whole loss
must be ours. Each must work on his own
account. True, that godly man who labours
so zealously to win your soul shall be a gainer
by your salvation; but your condemnation
will not lessen his merits or reward. That
friend for whom you have betrayed your conscience, that son whose interests you have
advanced at the cost of your soul, shall not
lessen the greatness of your loss.

What would you think of a man who
through neglect sacrificed his own fortune or
life while giving all his energies to the petty
concerns of a neighbour? Would you not
consider him a fool? And yet this is pre-
cisely what many who pass for sensible men
are doing. Rich men die leaving a splendid
inheritance to their children, and get credit
for having managed their affairs well. Their

affairs! say, rather, their children's. But how about their own? Their salvation, did they see to that? Alas, they had no time to think about it; death overtook them suddenly; they forgot themselves. While securing for a few years the worldly position of others, they have fixed their own in hell. *There is one that is wise and teacheth others, and yet is unprofitable to himself.*[1]

"'A debtor both to the wise and to the unwise:' owest thou nothing to thyself?"— *S. Bern.*

Stumbling-blocks.

WOE unto the world because of offences! Woe to that man by whom the offence cometh! It were better for him that a mill-stone were hanged about his neck, and that he were drowned in the depth of the sea.[2] Such is the malediction which the SAVIOUR utters. How terrible must the position of a man be which can be bettered by such a fate! The loss of an eye is a great misfortune, and yet according to our LORD, it becomes a positive advantage if we thus avoid being stumbling-blocks to others.

[1] Ecclus. xxxvii. 19.   [2] S. Matth. xviii. 7, 6.

You have stolen a piece of gold: there is no hope of salvation unless you make restitution. You have robbed your neighbour of innocence and purity, of charity, GOD's grace, and paradise: what atonement will you make? You have robbed your LORD of souls so precious to Him that He shed the last drop of His Blood to save them: how deeply He must feel the wrong! Can you hope for any mercy unless you do your utmost to repair it? The transports of joy felt by the SAVIOUR on finding the lost sheep, enable us to judge of His grief at its loss. Think you that He leaves unpunished a wrong which wounds Him to the quick? Doubt you that His grief will be the measure of His vengeance upon the author of His loss?

If you feel yourself guilty, whence comes it that you are at ease, and take so little trouble to make atonement and appease the wrath of GOD? Have you no fear of hearing such words as Cain heard: The blood of this innocent one, whom thou hast corrupted and deprived of the life of grace and utterly destroyed, crieth unto Me for vengeance; render an account of My blood which thou hast profaned by robbing it of its virtue: didst thou wish to show that thou hast more power to damn, than I to save a soul? Alas! what answer can you give to such reproaches? GOD has not counted the sacrifice of His own life too great to save a soul which you destroy, rather than forego the indulgence of a passing fancy! Can you lay claim to CHRIST's merits when you have marred their virtue?

"Every time he has set a bad example, he has added an item to his account."—*S. Aug.*

The Wickedness of Impurity.

MANY treat the sin of impurity as mere frailty, and in their blindness regard it as a light offence. And yet few sins are more grievous in themselves, none more fatal in their results. Impurity like fire burns deeply; nay, it is more fatal than fire in that the deeper it penetrates, the less is the injury felt and the more incurable it proves. It is that leaven which, appearing little, *leaveneth the whole lump.*[1] Like the almost unfelt sting of a snake, it instils its venom into the whole frame and gives the heart a deadly wound. Unless we fly from this snake, how can we

[1] Gal. v. 9.

escape being bitten? Unless we dread it, do we not deserve to perish?

Though other sins may be worse in themselves, none are more disastrous in their consequences. It is an unhappy property of impurity to multiply itself, and it may be said to be the cause of nearly all the greatest crimes which desolate the Christian world. Sacrilegious communions, public scandals, family divisions, slanders, blackest calumnies, strife, murder, parricide, poisonings, despair driving abandoned beings to destroy the cause or fruit of their sin by a still greater crime, abominable profanations of the holiest things —are the not uncommon results of what the world treats as frailty. Is such awful blindness not one of the most fatal fruits of this unhappy sin? Alas! does your small dread of it not show that you share this blindness, if not the sin which causes it?

Nothing will make you realize the heinousness of this sin so well as the light in which GOD views it. There is no sin which GOD has pardoned less or punished more. It has provoked the most awful vengeance ever inflicted by GOD on man. The waters of the flood, so Scripture declares, covered the earth to quench the flames of lust lighted in every heart. Four and twenty thousand Israelites were slain, to drown their sins in their own blood. The scourges inflicted on David for his adultery, so many souls consigned to perdition, prove that that cannot be a light offence which the All-merciful visits with such a terrible penalty, and that His judgment is very different from that of men.

" O mournful perversity, to sell to the devil, for a moment's pleasure, a soul bought with the Blood of CHRIST !"—*S. Aug.*

Occasions of Sin.

THE demon is not so formidable an adversary as we suppose. He can only attack the outworks of the heart; he cannot without we aid him, penetrate into the sanctuary. It is we who furnish him with weapons of offence. He owes his power to our weakness, or rather, to the rashness and readiness with which we are led into temptation. With less presumption we should prove stronger, and he weaker ; he would have less hold upon us, did we not ourselves give it by courting the presence of sin.

The demon cannot storm or surprise the

citadel of the heart except by tampering with the garrison, that is to say, our affections. He tries to gain them over by placing before them some interest, the attraction of some pleasure, or the glitter of some distinction. Such things affect but little at a distance, but, when circumstances present them before us, they powerfully influence our senses and affections. These, once gained over, corrupt the reason, and bring the will *into captivity to the law of sin.*[1]

Men are for the most part moulded by the influences which surround them. They turn out good or bad according to circumstances. The reason is this : External objects breed thoughts ; thoughts in turn desires ; and desires affections—and our affections make our vices or virtues. It is opportunity which lends them power over us. Avoid these occasions of sin if you would avoid sinning. This is the easiest and surest means. Fear, and thou shalt be safe; fly, and thou shalt win the fight.

" A gracious Providence has made victory depend on fear and flight."—*S. Cypr.*

[1] Rom. vii. 23.

The Perils of Lukewarmness.

THE state of the lukewarm is full of peril.
It often renders us the objects of GOD's
judgments by making us resist His merciful
designs. There are persons towards whom
GOD cherishes a special affection, and whose
path is watched by a special providence.
Blessed with a virtuous nature, a happy disposition, a noble spirit, a good heart, a sound
judgment, they are prevented with abundant
grace, and stung with remorse for the least
fault. Such persons cannot be mere average
Christians. They must belong to GOD altogether, or not at all. They must be saints,
or they will be reprobates. JESUS does not
spare His Apostles. He tells them that unless
their humility be deep, like that of little children, they cannot hope to be saved. They
were not allowed to be average Christians.
Possibly, it was the attempt to be one that
turned an Apostle into an Apostate.

Lukewarmness is dangerous, because it is
a state of blindness caused by the frequent
commission of trifling faults, by want of
recollectedness, and by our ruling passion
blinding us to the sins which enslave us.
Thus we erect a false standard, and grave

offences are reckoned light faults. Envenomed animosities are treated as antipathy or indifference, cruel slanders as pleasantries, sinful murmurings as just complaints, dangerous diversions as innocent pleasures, improper intimacies as honest friendships, licentious liberties as harmless frolic. Nothing is thought of a life of perpetual uselessness, of a self-indulgence reaching idolatry, of a frame of mind which affects ignorance of the plainest duties, and carefully avoids being enlightened concerning them.

Once more, lukewarmness is dangerous, because in a manner incurable. It is easier to convert a great sinner than a lukewarm professor. A soul thus blinded ignores both the disease and its consequences, and therefore betakes itself not to the proper remedy. Its case resembles that of persons in delicate health, in whom some vital organ is secretly affected. Such persons, because they do not suffer much, and live like their neighbours, are blind to their danger, neglect the proper remedies, and are brought to their graves before they have realised that they are ill. Similarly the lukewarm, because they can show some good works, and commit no gross (though none the less grievous) sins, either seek no remedy for a disease of which they see not the consequences, or the ill-success of the means hitherto tried makes them loath to try them again, or the remedies themselves have lost their power and are of no avail.

"I have seen the cold and carnal become hot and spiritual, but the lukewarm barely ever."—*Cassian.*

The Tendency of little Sins.

NO man ever became wholly wicked all at once. There are few who do not at first look with horror upon a crime. Whatever the corruption lodged in the heart by original sin, whatever the disorder it has produced in the spirit, it has still left some scattered seeds of righteousness compelling us to condemn great crimes in the case of others, and inspiring a dread of committing them ourselves. But by familiarizing themselves with venial sin, which always bears a relation to mortal, men little by little are less startled by it; then they view it with less detestation; soon they do not fear it so much; it is witnessed in others with small indignation or surprise; it has lost its terrible, it has even acquired an attractive look; until at length it is committed without compunction, nay, even with pleasure. These are the steps leading over the precipice.

The commission of venial sin is a going astray, not final apostasy, yet those who are continually going astray end in being lost. It does not indicate an entire estrangement from GOD, but a growing cold which predisposes to it. Those who, by venial sin, accustom themselves to neglect GOD come by degrees to despise Him. Genuine love does not become hatred all at once, but weak love soon turns to indifference, indifference to coldness, and coldness to hatred or contempt. Slipping down the precipice almost insensibly, the sinner scarcely notices his fall until he has gone so far as to render it very difficult to recover himself. Alas! am I not in danger of falling blindly into this pitiful state myself? Suffer it not, LORD, but open mine eyes, and vouchsafe me strength to escape so great a calamity.

" From venial men rush onwards to deadly sins."—*S. Bern.*

Œhe Use of Affliction.

OUR misfortunes and disgraces are often mercies, and what we look upon as effects of GOD's wrath the clearest proofs of His tender love. Sufferings cause us to retire into ourselves, because we find nothing satisfying abroad. They wean us from self by humiliations : for how feel self-satisfied when spurned and despised ? they wean us from the world : for how cling to an impostor that has first flattered and then betrayed ? and they wean us from sin, by rekindling that faith which teaches us that our sorrows are the consequences and penalties of sin. Is it not, then, an act of love to procure us such advantages ; to enable us to show GOD our love and earn His in turn ? Every other proof of our love for GOD is uncertain and deceptive ; this one alone is infallible. Those who only love and serve Him in prosperity are no better than Jews, but those who love and serve in the furnace of affliction are true Christians.

Again, is there no love in enabling us to strengthen, through practice, our habits of virtue. A virtue cannot be acquired unless it be practised, and when is there a better opportunity for practising patience, gentleness, self-denial, humility, charity, and conformity to GOD's will than amid sufferings? They are at once the most efficacious means of acquiring virtues, the surest signs of their genuineness, and the strongest proofs of their strength.

Once more, is not that love which enables us to become like CHRIST in His crucifixion, in order that we may hereafter be like Him in His glory? Not love, which furnishes us with occasions of increasing our reward, of adding lustre to our crown, and of gaining as many additional degrees of glory as there have been moments in our lives consecrated by suffering? Can we have a greater proof of the reality and greatness of GOD's love? can we give a sadder proof of our ingratitude than when we make His greatest favours subjects of murmuring and sorrow? Would it not be a fitting punishment, were we to be spared and left to ourselves?

" If our very chastisement are favours, what shall the favours be when He hath ceased to chasten?"—*S. Aug.*

The Omnipotence of Prayer.

THE virtue of prayer must needs be infallible since it rests on the goodness of GOD and the faithfulness and merits of JESUS CHRIST. Before it can prove ineffectual, when duly offered, GOD's goodness or the faithfulness and merits of CHRIST must fail. The property of infinite goodness is to communicate itself without measure : what then may we not expect? It is a sun which irradiates the whole universe without losing a particle of its own brightness; it is an immeasurable fulness which seeks to fill every void. Open then your heart by prayer, and it shall be filled. Humble prayer is the avowal of our want and weakness; it both creates the void and enables us to have it filled. CHRIST has not only promised but sworn that we shall obtain all that we ask in His name. Needed He to swear with an oath before we would believe? What an honour GOD does us when He swears for our sakes; what a dishonour we do Him when we distrust His oath! And do we not seem to distrust it when we pray with so much timidity and so little confidence? The Church asks everything through JESUS CHRIST; He asks with us what we ask through Him. The FATHER can refuse Him nothing, since He has a right to ask that which His mercy has merited for us. The eternal FATHER owes us everything because the SON has given everything for us. He cannot give us too much because His power cannot reach further than the merits of His SON. If, then, we remain poor with so inexhaustible a Treasury to draw upon, must not the fault be ours?

" Prayer is omnipotent: single-handed it can do anything."—*Theod.*

Neighbourly Love.

GOD in the Law commanded men to love their neighbours. In the Gospel JESUS reiterates this command. In His discourse at the Last Supper, when He was as it were making His Will, He repeats it thrice to mark how much He has its observance at heart. He assures us that this is in a special manner His commandment. It is that which He had oftenest taught by His example, all other virtues being but the fruits of this one. It is the special feature and essence of the New Covenant. By it must His disciples be known.

Not by the working of miracles, not by the gift of tongues, not by faith itself—others who are none of His shall have these—but by brotherly love alone shall they be recognized. Dost thou, then, discern this feature in thyself? Bearest thou this character stamped upon thee? Thou mayst have faith enough to move mountains, courage enough to undergo martyrdom, and yet without this thou art not CHRIST's disciple. Thou hast not His spirit because thou hast not charity. He assures us that the commandment of the love of our neighbour is like unto that of the love of GOD—like, because identical both in principle and object. What makes me love GOD for Himself, makes me love my neighbour for GOD's sake. I cannot love GOD unless I love my neighbour.

"Lovest thou Him whose precept thou contemnest?"—*S. Aug.*

The Excellence of God's Will.

SIN is the only evil which GOD wills not, but yet He wills its results. He condemned the envy of Joseph's brethren, but yet He willed its result—Joseph's servitude.

The fury of the Jews filled Him with horror, but yet He willed and ordained the death of His Son. And in like manner He will punish the wrong which thou art suffering, but yet He wills the loss and affliction which it causeth thee. We may indeed regret such evils when viewed merely by themselves, but how shall we murmur against the will of God? It is God's will. Ah! solemn words! What further reasons does a man need who believes and loves God? Dare a Christian say, God wills this, but I will it not?

The Will of God, being infinitely wise, does everything for the best, and chooses the best means of arriving at its end. The aim of all His works is His Glory: can He want zeal to procure, or light to know, or power to use the proper means? In carrying out His designs He can draw light out of darkness, and use the most unlikely instruments. He destroyed sin in the world by the worst of sins— Deicide. Let us then adore His inscrutable designs, and believe that He orders all things for the best, and can do more than we can comprehend.

Not only does the Will of God do all for the best in the abstract, but for us individually. Shall we then fear to abandon ourselves to His guidance? He is our FATHER—more than a father—can His strokes be otherwise than salutary? He heals when He seems to hurt; He weans us from the creature to win us to Himself; He secures our eternal when He seems to forget our temporal welfare. And yet, while dreading impediments to our prosperity here, we calmly risk the shipwreck of our souls!

"Give me what Thou wilt, and how much Thou wilt, and when Thou wilt."—*De imit. Christi.*

Zeal.

THE world shall henceforth teach me how to serve GOD. The conduct of worldlings shall be my example and rule; I will learn of them how zealously I ought to serve. What will they not do, what not suffer, to please the world? and yet, even when they succeed, where is their profit? To please GOD, on the other hand, I need only entertain the wish, to be abundantly rewarded. In the often fruitless endeavour to gain the world's favour, welfare, peace, honour, conscience, salvation—all is freely sacrificed; and yet I will not sacrifice to GOD the least interest or pleasure! Can the strictest observance of religious duties, or the severest exercises of penitential discipline be compared with the ready subservience of a courtier, or the sufferings and hardships of a soldier? How disgraceful is it that we should do less for God than the world's followers for it—less for our salvation than they for their perdition! The thought of hell ought surely to quicken our zeal. Shall we count any task too laborious which can save us from eternal fire? We sear with a hot iron a wound which endangers life; what ought we not to endure, then, when eternity is at stake? The thought, too, of heaven ought to stimulate us; no sacrifice should appear too costly which is to gain for us eternal bliss. Can anything stir us up more to do all the good we can, than the thought that the most indifferent action, when done for God, earns for us the possession of Him; and that our recompense in heaven shall be exactly proportional to the zeal with which we have employed every moment of our lives in some useful work? If a merchant had a limited time allowed him to realize enormous profits, would he lose a single moment?

" Be as zealous for the world's Maker as thou hast been for the world."—*S. Aug.*

Salvation our own Business.

TO secure our salvation is the only business which we can strictly call our
own, because it is almost the only one which
cannot be done for us, or, at least, without
our help. Nearly everything else can be done
by proxy. You may be engaged in a lawsuit
and little versed in legal matters, but by the
help of competent advisers the suit may be
gained without your active interference. A
king may be an indifferent captain, and yet
win battles through his lieutenants without
running any personal risk. Not so with your
salvation. Here there can be no deputy.
You have a fierce campaign before you, powerful enemies,—the world and the demon.
You have no lieutenant, no representative ;
you must fight in person if you wish to be
victorious. You are to be tried before a Judge
as perfectly wise as He is upright ; on His
judgment depends eternal blessedness or eternal misery; you must, were you monarch of
the universe, appear in person and plead your
own cause.

In other matters, much as we may rely on
the talents and zeal of friends, we rely still

more on our own. We naturally think we shall manage them best, being the most interested parties. And, however much we may seek the support of Providence in our temporal concerns, we think ourselves bound to second it with our own efforts. In the matter of salvation alone do we leave all to God, as if He could do everything and we nothing. And yet He can effect everything without our co-operation except this one thing—our salvation. We cannot indeed be saved without His grace, but His grace cannot save us without our active assistance. To believe the contrary is a fatal error; to live as though one believed it, is not faith but presumption,

"God made, but He cannot save thee without thy help."—*S. Aug.*

Fidelity to Grace.

GRACE is the voice of God speaking to us: with what a loving, teachable spirit should we listen; He is then visiting us: how humbly and respectfully should we receive Him; He is come in search of us:

how gratefully should we go and meet Him! And, if we heed not His voice, welcome not His visits, open not the door when He knocks, how great the indignity and ingratitude! And yet this is what we do each time that we are faithless to grace. How terribly GOD will punish such contempt! If we will not hear, He will cease to speak,—a silence more awful than the loudest menace; if we will not welcome, He will withdraw,—a calamity greater than the heaviest chastisement; if we repel Him, He will abandon us,—the severest penalty He can inflict.

Grace is the price of the Blood of CHRIST, the fruit of His death. If it be the price of His Blood, how should we prize it; if the fruit of His passion and death, how should we hoard it! To resist grace is to tread under foot the Blood of CHRIST. Shall not that Blood trodden under foot cry louder than the blood of Abel (not for mercy, as it would have done had we valued it, but) for vengeance against Its profaners? If the principle of our life, the foundation of our hopes becomes the occasion of our condemnation, the instrument of our ruin: what resource is left? What can we be but reprobates? Grace is accompanied by every blessing; when we lose grace we lose everything.

" It is our part to yield to grace, it is GOD's to reward us for yielding."—*S. Aug.*

𝕭𝖊𝖘𝖊𝖙𝖙𝖎𝖓𝖌 𝕾𝖎𝖓𝖘.

FEW are without some besetting sin. The most virtuous are not those who have none, but who combat it best. It must be known, it must be conquered. If it be not, it will conquer us. There can be no truce with this enemy. Victory alone can purchase peace and with it our salvation. This sin is the source of almost all our other sins; we must cut off the head of this Goliath if we would vanquish the rest of the Philistines; their total defeat depends on that of this redoubted enemy. The victory will be dearly won, but it will well repay all our efforts.

The besetting sin prevents our knowing the other sins which it makes us commit, or at least their enormity. All sin blinds, but especially the besetting sin. All that we eagerly desire appears right to us, saith S. Augustine. The dominant passion seduces the reason, veils, if it does not extinguish, its light. Well founded doubts are treated as scruples; a false standard of right and wrong are bolstered up by a self-adopted code of morality; and we cheat ourselves into thinking that we can compound for our own by a display of indignation against the sins of others. The covetous man cannot understand how the unchaste can lead so scandalous a life: such a man must be surely lost: but he has no difficulty in understanding how men can steal and retain the property of others, and fatten on the wages of unrighteousness. The unchaste, again, cannot conceive how a man can rob the widow and the orphans, such hard and unrighteous conduct he thinks cannot hope for mercy,—but he does not waste a thought upon the innocent girl whom he has brutally sacrificed to his lusts. He confidently relies on the mercy of GOD, because, forsooth, with all his frailty, he at least compassionates the sorrows of others!

This reigning passion, by blinding us to the disorders it entails, of necessity renders all escape impossible, and bars the way to repentance; no remedy is sought for an unfelt evil. Moreover this sin is the principle of almost all our actions. It enters into all our thoughts and aims. Strengthened by being so often brought into play, it becomes a habit, and then a necessity. As a matter of fact, how few persons do we see give up a besetting sin or an inveterate habit? Art thou not still the slave of that sin which held thee captive twenty years ago? Nay, hath it not tightened its grasp? It shall rule thee through life; it shall accompany thee through the gate of death into the grave; it shall lead thee down to hell.

"An evil wish becomes a ruling passion; and then an imperious necessity."—*S. Aug.*

Recreation a Remedy.

RECREATIONS are remedies vouchsafed by God for the relief of our infirmities. Being remedies, they must not be injurious, dangerous, or continuous. Not injurious, as is the case with sinful pleasures; for is it not fearful blindness to rest one's happiness on what some day must be bitterly repented of, if it is not to prove the cause of unspeakable misery and eternal condemnation? Does that deserve the name of pleasure which is leading us on to so fatal an end? Not dangerous: for, although most pastimes would be innocent if we were innocent ourselves, the corrupt heart instils a subtle venom into what appears least noxious, and we find poison in our very remedies, and destruction in the things which were intended by GOD to subserve our welfare and relieve our weakness. No sensible man would willingly risk his life by trying a hazardous remedy : what then are we to think of those who time after time, of their own accord, take part in recreations which, innocent in themselves, have been proved by experience to be full of danger ? Are you not running this risk daily, and have you no fear of its proving fatal ? Not excessive or continuous : for remedies cease to be remedies when taken too frequently or in too large quantities. A ceaseless round of pleasures enervates the heart, weakens the mind, and by inducing a state of self-indulgent indolence, renders the simplest duties irksome and distasteful. Pleasures are intended to rest the body and relax the mind : have those persons any need of repose, who never do anything, or of relaxation, whose whole life is a comedy ?

" Wine is as good as life to a man, if it be drunk moderately."—*Ecclus.*

The Sinfulness of Slander.

THERE is nothing more common in so-
ciety than slander. Light though this
sin appears to many, it is none the less grievous. Men call it jesting, fun, wit; GOD
gives it another name. Is it not blindness to
regard that as a light sin which banishes from
Heaven, which directly attacks the foremost
virtue, charity; which robs a neighbour of
his honour, that is to say, of that which all
ought to value above every earthly gift, and
which many wise and generous spirits prefer
to life itself? Theft and homicide are light
offences if slander be not a grievous one.
They often do less harm. S. James calls
slander *a world of iniquity*,[1] to show that it is
the source of an infinite number of sins,—
can it then be a light offence?

The slanderer, says S. Bernard, inflicts
three mortal wounds at one stroke. He
wounds himself by destroying charity, the life
of the soul. He wounds the slandered by
blighting his good name, and inspiring un-
christian resentment. He wounds, lastly, the
bystander by instilling the poison into his ears

[1] S. James iii. 6.

and making him an accomplice through his curiosity and readiness to listen, or cowardice in allowing such language to remain unchastised. The more subtle and disguised the slander, the less culpable is it thought. But does the arrow pierce the less deeply for being sharply pointed? does the adder sting less dangerously when it is coiled amid flowers? does poison cease to be poison when disguised in some pleasant drink? And shall the weapons of slander cut the less keenly to the quick, or wound less deadly for being sharp and polished?

It is a cowardly vice, the offspring of a craven spirit, a kind of assassination. It does not attack openly, there would be a risk in that, so it lies in ambush. It attacks unawares those who cannot defend themselves or parry its thrusts. Worse still, it often attacks the innocent, and those from whom it has never suffered wrong. What excuse can be made for a man who hurts another without cause, stabbing him in cold blood with a smile upon his face?

Treachery is often added to cowardice. The victim is caressed and flattered at the very moment that he is pierced to the quick; pitied while pulled to pieces; commended while decried. The slander is seasoned with

faint praise to render it more probable, and its
shaft more sure. From double tongues, good
LORD, deliver us !

" A word is easily shot, wounds easily, but
is not easily withdrawn."—*S. Bern.*

Paradise.

WHAT is Paradise? It is a region whose
inhabitants have none other portion
than GOD Himself, but who, in possessing
Him, possesses all things. In Paradise we
shall see GOD face to face, there shall be
no veil; possess Him securely, because we
shall never fear to lose Him ; love Him cease-
lessly, perfectly, wholly, because He shall
fill our hearts ; rejoice in Him without satiety,
because in Him we shall ever find fresh beau-
ties, ever taste fresh pleasures. Seeing and
possessing, we shall grow like Him,—holy,
pure, wise, mighty ; transformed, we shall
have the same wills, affections, and desires.
All to us, we shall find all in Him.

He alone, SAVIOUR, who could realise Thy
nature and excellency, could comprehend the
bliss which is being prepared for them that

love Thee. Thou alone canst conceive it; Thou alone hast merited it; Thou alone canst enable me to possess it. When, O Jesus, shall I enjoy that blessedness of which Thou art the Source and Object? when behold Thee face to face, not as in a glass darkly? when wilt Thou fill my soul with that torrent of delight which refreshes Thy holy city?

"We shall enjoy but One; but that One shall be everything to us."—*S. Aug.*

Conversion delayed.

WHEN you delay your conversion, saith S. Bernard, you believe either that GOD will not pardon you, or that He will. If you believe that He will not, what folly it is to offend a mighty enemy without hope of pardon, and swell your punishment by swelling the number of your sins! If you believe that GOD is so merciful that He will never —no matter how frequent your offences— weary of forgiving, what black ingratitude to make *that* a cause of offending Him, which should only increase your love! How strange

F

it is, says Tertullian, to argue thus,—God is good, so I must be wicked ; He will pardon and spare, so I will offend Him without fear ; He will be long-suffering and patient, so I will insult Him by going on in sin ! Is a Christian—is unregenerate man—capable of reasoning thus ?

If you believe that God will give you little time for working out your conversion, why do you not make the most of moments so brief and precious ? If you believe that He will give you much, how deep should be your gratitude ! and how can you prove it better than by spending the opportunities vouchsafed to you, in appeasing His anger and learning to love Him ? How great then is your ingratitude and wickedness when you employ them in sin ! And yet such is the case whenever conversion is delayed.

Once more, if you do not believe that you will some day repent of the sins which you keep committing, you are without hope and without God ; but if you do, what madness to derive pleasure from things of which you must repent, if you would not perish,—which must be bewailed here or eternally hereafter ! If sin retains its sweetness up to the grave, it will result in everlasting bitterness ; and if, happily, penitence betimes turns it into wormwood, how can you take any pleasure in an act which must then fill you with the utmost pain ?

" I had found the precious pearl .... and I hesitated to buy it !"—*S. Aug.*

Repentance must bear Fruits.

BRING forth fruits meet for repentance,[1] said the Baptist to the Jews of old. He says the same to-day to Christians. Each word is significant. We must " bring forth fruits,"—not merely talk about repentance. In the present day there is plenty of talk about it, but where are its fruits? Certain penitential forms are repeated in which the heart bears no part,—mere words and nothing more ! Men protest that they wish to be changed and converted, but nothing is done, —mere words ! What are such words but empty wind? What can they do for sin? Such persons resemble the fig-tree, mentioned in the Gospel, which had leaves, but nothing else. They have leaves to cover and deceive themselves and others,—the appearance of repentance. There is much self-accusation ; much pleading for pardon ; many a promise

[1] S. Matth. iii. 8.

made and never kept,—mere leaves. Is their
heart touched? is their sorrow sincere? is
their determination to forsake sin carried out?
Nothing of the kind.

There are others who, not satisfied with
bearing leaves only, bring forth the flowers too
of penitence. They appear touched; shed a
few tears; make a few efforts. These are
flowers which seem to give promise of coming
fruits. But they are soon blighted by the
pestilent atmosphere of the world with its, ensnaring influences and pleasures, and the apparently well-grounded hopes of an abundance
of fruits dispelled.

Once more, it is not enough to bring forth
fruits. The fruits must be *meet for repentance*.[1]
They must be proportionate to the Majesty
of our offended GOD; to the greatness and
frequency of our sins; and to the wilfulness
and ingratitude which we have displayed.
And if so, does a light and imperfect repentance like ours bear any proportion to the dishonour we have done GOD? do we measure
the heinous malignity of our offences by the
few short prayers which we hurriedly repeat?

"Let your penitence bear some proportion
to your sin."—*S. Cypr.*

---

[1] S. Matth. iii. 8.

Relapses into Sin.

WHENCE is it that you are perpetually falling back into the same sins? Is it not because you will not make use of the proper precautions? And why not? Because you are not resolutely determined to break with your sins. Those who are, use the necessary means. Do you think a sick man really wishes to be cured when he will take no remedies? and is your case not similar? Can one believe that you really desire the cure of your soul, when you neglect nearly all the means prescribed?

Some remedies you might, perhaps, be induced to try, but not those recommended, not those suitable to your case. They appear too violent; you call them irksome. All this proves that you are not steadfastly resolved to forsake sin. Will you have a proof? If asked to employ these remedies for some violent bodily disorder, would you hesitate a moment? would they not appear simple? Whence comes it then that they appear impracticable where your conversion is concerned, if it be not because in the one case you are in earnest, and in the other you are not? But to desire your conversion after this fashion, is equivalent to not desiring it at all ; for so feeble a desire is incapable of producing genuine repentance.

But, say some, the obstacles are greater than the remedies, and this is the reason why we fall back into sin. But what are these obstacles? Some passion ; your relations with some person ; some occasion of temptation. Have you ever taken effectual means to overcome them? Have you ever made a serious effort to conquer that passion which is enticing and drawing you into temptation? Are you not carried away after making little or no resistance? These obstacles are, no doubt, great ; but if your goods, your health, or some lawsuit, were at stake, they would not overpower you as they do when you are called upon to avoid sin—and why? Simply because your will is determined in the former, but not in the latter case. Remember, however, that your penitence is not real if unaccompanied by a firm resolution to give up sin.

"Penitence is vain when sin dogs its steps."
—*S. Aug.*

Judicial Blindness of Heart.

MENTAL and spiritual blindness is the most common cause of sin. Every sinner is blind ; he is a sinner simply because he is blind. If he had a real knowledge of GOD, of himself, and of sin, he would never commit it. Knowing the greatness, goodness, and righteousness of GOD, could he despise, hate, and insult Him ? Knowing his own vileness, misery, and weakness, could he prefer himself to his Maker, as he does every time that he falls into deadly sin ? Knowing the fearful nature of sin, how hateful, how fatal it is, could he love it more than GOD ? Could he after thoroughly realizing the infinite calamities which follow in its wake make it his sovereign good ? LORD, let me receive my sight ; open mine eyes, enlighten my understanding, cure my blindness ; let me see Thy mercies, and love them ; my own abject misery, and loathe it ; the hideousness of sin, and hate and avoid it.

Again, blindness is the effect as well as the cause of sin—its offspring as well as its parent. When sin enters the heart, it extinguishes the light. The first man enjoyed at his creation

an abundance of light. Sin closed his eyes.
Having aspired to a knowledge which was
not good for him, he was condemned to ignorance and error. How comes it that men are
so enlightened and prudent in other respects,
and yet so ignorant and blind as regards the
saving truths of the Gospel? It is because
they are sinners. Enlightened and clever on
every other question, they are fools and babes,
in the science of salvation. And yet what
shall everything else profit a man if he knows
not how to save his soul?

Blindness is an awful penalty of sin. The
sinner *loves darkness rather than light.*[1] God
to punish him, consigns him to it. He cannot chastise him more terribly than by granting
what he desires. The sinner delights in
darkness: God makes it the instrument of his
punishment. The small concern you feel
about your soul is a sign of blindness. The
greater the blindness of the heart, the less it is
realized : this is the reason why you feel so
easy about yourself.

" God sheds judicial blindness over lawless
lusts."—*S. Aug.*

[1] S. John iii. 19.

Self-Surrender to God's Guidance.

HAPPY the soul which abandons itself to the conduct of GOD! It feels sure that GOD will never leave nor forsake it, though every creature may. When GOD guides and protects, what can harm?

The perfection of self-surrender to the conduct of GOD is shown in its practice where it appears most contrary to our interests and inclinations. Our principal, or rather our one desire must be to follow the will of GOD. And this must be done, even where we see not the reason. The will of GOD is reason enough: any additional reason rather weakens the merit by weakening the absoluteness of the surrender. All is not given to GOD when we *reason* ourselves into giving. Entire self-surrender asks not the question, Why? Nay more, absolute self-surrender abandons itself to GOD's conduct even *against* reason. Faith never shines more brightly than when it believes truths which it not only cannot test, but which are contrary to the evidence of the senses and the conclusions of reason. How admirable is this self-surrender! How it condemns our vain disquietudes, wilful eagerness, groundless fears, and over-caution! Surrender we all to GOD, and we shall find all in GOD.

" Cast thyself on Him: He will not withdraw and let thee fall."—*S. Aug.* .

Faithfulness in little Things.

'TIS a trifle, you say, an unimportant rule, a little grace,—what does it matter? Nothing is a trifle in connection with so great a Being as GOD ; nothing, which can please or displease Him ; nothing, which can help or hinder our perfection and salvation, or even add or subtract a single degree of eternal glory. It is not a little thing to be faithful in little things. It is a mark of great love to wish to please in everything, to displease in nothing, however trivial, Him we love. If you are waiting for great occasions of working in GOD's service, when will you work? How rare those great occasions! The SON of GOD hath Himself declared, *He that is faithful in that which is least, is faithful also in much ; and he that is unjust in the least, is unjust also in much.*[1]

---

[1] S. Luke xvi. 10.

The greatest conflagrations often originate in a spark; the deadliest sins, in some trifling fault; a man's reprobation, in some grace despised. Besides, if the thing be a trifle, your negligence is the less excusable. The difficulty of a thing may be a pretext for faint-heartedness, but its easiness can never excuse neglect. *If*, said the servants of Naaman, *the prophet had bid thee do some great thing, wouldst thou not have done it? How much rather, then, when he saith to thee, Wash and be clean.*[1] After all that JESUS has done and suffered for us, would it not be cowardice to shrink from the most arduous tasks He might lay upon us? How much less can their neglect be excused when light and easy?

"Despise not little things, or thou shalt never do great ones."—*S. Jerome.*

Lively Faith.

FAITH without works only justifies GOD when He condemns us. *He that believeth not is condemned already;*[2] but he that believes and acts not in accordance with his faith shall

[1] 2 Kings v. 13.   [2] S. John iii. 18.

be still more condemned. The barren fig tree is cut down and cast into the fire; the unprofitable servant who has buried his talent is cast into outer darkness. CHRIST gives no other reason for the condemnation of nominal Christians in the day of judgment than the omission of works of mercy. *I was an hungred, and ye gave Me no meat,* shall be said to those who *shall go away into everlasting punishment.*[1]

Do good then. Not to do it is to do evil. A useless life is a sinful life. Act up to the measure of your light. According to the light shall be the rigour of the judgment. Do as much good as you have done evil, and you will do much. Do all the good you can. Limit the good you do, and you limit your love.to GOD, and His goodness to you. Do good zealously, for *cursed is he that doeth the work of the Lord deceitfully.*[2] Do it with a pure intention, else good becomes evil, light changes into darkness. Do it with the help of grace, else it will have no merit. And when you have done all, say, *We are unprofitable servants: we have done that which was our duty to do.*[3] How many persons have leaves without fruit, the appearance of virtue without the reality! How many mistake the

---

[1] S. Matth. xxv. 42, 45. [2] Jer. xlviii. 10.
[3] S. Luke xvii. 10.

results of a happy temperament, a careful education, a worldly sense of honour, the desire of men's praise, at best, a heathen morality, for the fruits of holiness! How many, innocent in their own eyes, because the world can bring no charge against them, live soft and useless lives, neither acquiring virtues, nor practising works of mercy!

" The life is not idle when the heart is busy."—*S. Ambr.*

Reliance on God.

WE cannot trust God, or distrust ourselves too much. He never denies the petition of lively faith; our confidence is the measure of His gifts. The reason is plain: trust is a proof of love—it always exists between the loving and the loved. Besides, there cannot be a better proof of our sense of His goodness, power, wisdom, and foresight.

Alone I can do nothing: how not distrust myself? God helping me, I can do anything: how not trust in Him? Hence was it that the prophet declared: *They that wait upon*

G

the Lord shall renew their strength ; they shall mount up with wings as eagles; they shall run and not be weary, and they shall walk and not faint.[1] If then you lack strength, it is because you lack trust.

As the power of GOD is never so conspicuous as when it gathers light out of darkness, and brings the most marvellous works out of nothing : so faith shines brightest when the very motives for despair are made so many reasons for hope, when like Abraham, a man hopes against hope. A man thus upheld, never fears less than when he has everything to fear; never hopes more than when his circumstances are desperate ; never abandons himself more unreservedly to GOD'S care than when every one, apparently GOD Himself, has abandoned him. It is then that he says with Job, *Though He slay me, yet will I trust in Him;*[2] yes, I will lean on the arm that smites me. However great the evils threatened, nothing is more to be feared than faithless fear.

" The faith of Christians is a faith in the impossible."—*Tert.*

[1] Isa. xl. 31.　　[2] Job xiii. 15.

On loving Christ.

CHRIST longs for our love! Is this not in itself a sufficient motive for loving Him? It is as difficult to conceive of a GOD eagerly desiring our love as it is to conceive our being capable of refusing it. Can our love add anything, can the loss of it subtract anything from His happiness? And yet He does not hesitate to proclaim this eager longing. It is shown in the tenderness with which the Beloved calls His Spouse, as well as in His thrice-repeated inquiry, whether Peter loved Him.

He leaves nothing undone to obtain His desire. He invites by promises, He appeals to self-interest, excites by favours, solicits by prayers, yea, compels by commands, and constrains by threats. All His works in the order of nature and grace have this for their end. Which then is the most incomprehensible—His eager importunity, or our stubborn resistance?

His longing for our love is a plain proof of exceeding great love for us: while the faintness of our desire to love, is as plain a proof that we love Him not. Did we love, we should feel how worthy He is of love, and long to love more; feel pained at our lack of love, and eagerly embrace every means of augmenting it; the hardest ways would become easy in our eyes, and we should exclaim at every moment, Thy love, JESUS, Thy love and nothing else. Alas, how far removed am I from feeling that perfect love! Thou only, my SAVIOUR, canst at once give me this ardent desire, and enable me to love Thee truly.

"Thou, LORD, commandest me to love Thee: grant what Thou commandest, and command what Thou wilt."—*S. Aug.*

How God's Will must be done.

OUR perfection consists not in praying, working, fasting, or winning souls, but in doing GOD's will. Such acts however excellent in themselves, if they be not ordained of GOD are disorderly; if not animated by this motive, are imperfect. The best actions become faulty, if not done in the order prescribed by GOD, and the most indifferent become excellent when done according to His will. It is not always seasonable to practise penitence, or mortification, to pray, or labour, but it is, to do GOD's will. And we do it when we keep His commandments, follow the motions of grace, do our duty in our state of life, and *obey them that have the rule over*[1] us.

Again, it is not enough to do GOD's will; we must do it in the way He wills. To do GOD's will, but not as He wills, is to do right in the wrong way, and so not do it at all. We perform an action in a way pleasing to GOD when we join to it all the accompaniments which constitute the perfection of an action. First, we must do it at the proper time: to pray when we are required to work, to talk when we should keep silence, is not to do GOD's will. Secondly, we must do it where GOD wills: a mistress at church when she should be superintending her household, a priest in his parish when he should be in his closet, is not doing right in the right place. Thirdly, it must be done in the way GOD likes, that is, with prudence and fervour: done in a careless or perfunctory way, the reward is forfeited.

Once more we must do what is right, for the sole reason that GOD wills it. This must be our only, or at least first motive. In this way the meanest actions become supernatural, and the holiest still more perfect. It is a

[1] Heb. xiii. 17.

G 2

short and sure way of becoming holy : happy he who follows it ! When therefore the doing of GOD's will jumps with your interests or pleasures, avert your eyes from the latter, and fasten them on it. For example, husbands and wives must love each other, and their offspring ; but they must not be moved by natural affection alone, or by reason alone, that is to act as heathens or philosophers, they must look first to GOD's will.

" Made for Thee, the heart knows no rest until it finds Thee."—*S. Aug.*

God's Service, our Glory.

NO action is so glorious as that of glorifying GOD. To serve so mighty a Master is to reign. GOD alone is great. We think other things great simply because we ourselves are pigmies. The glory of the greatest conquerors, what is it but an empty shadow? What then are those paltry interests which we are daily setting before GOD's glory ? Rest assured that the prayer of faith, humiliation patiently endured, seasonable self-mortification; a work of mercy, any good deed done for GOD's sake and to promote His glory, is a greater and more splendid achievement than the most important transactions, and the government or conquest of an empire. Do you believe this? Alas! if you did, would you so readily omit your religious duties, perform them so reluctantly, be so negligent in all that promotes GOD's glory? If you are ambitious, here is the field for its exercise. What would you say of one who, charged with the burden of an empire, spent his time, like that eccentric Roman emperor, in chasing flies? and is your folly less? You are born to a work which has occupied GOD from all eternity—His glory and your salvation —and yet you stoop to frivolous pursuits, and waste your time on a thousand nothings which, however the blindness of self-deceit may magnify them, are only fit to amuse children.

"A little man must he be who reckons anything great except the one, eternal, infinite, Good."—*De imit. Christi.*

The Blessedness of Repentance.

THOUGH penitence wears a stern aspect, telling of temptations and conflicts, of wounds and tears, it is not after all so harsh as it appears. If it has its severities, it has also its sweets; if ever accompanied by pangs, it is often followed by still greater consolations. Its tears are not always bitter; and a sinner often finds greater satisfaction in bewailing his sins than he ever found in committing them. True, he has battles to fight, but the confident expectation of victory sustains him; and if the warfare is against self, it is a saving warfare ending in a blessed peace. If it be *an evil thing and bitter* to *forsake the Lord,*[1] as saith the prophet Jeremiah, it is sweet to seek Him with the hope of finding Him through repentance. If it is a sad thought to a penitent that he has irritated Him and exposed himself to all the consequences of His wrath, it is a very sweet one that the SAVIOUR compassionates his tears, and grants him that pardon which is never refused to *a broken and contrite heart.* If it is sad to be agitated by the motions of unruly passions, frightened at the sight of past sins, and stung with remorse, it is very sweet to see sins blotted out, remorse allayed by sorrowing penitence, and the tempest of ungoverned passions succeeded by peace and the triumph of grace.

[1] Jer. ii. 19.

But when to all these sweets of penitence, which moderate its severity so much, the SAVIOUR imparts, as He often does, His purest consolations; when He takes pleasure in shedding over the soul, along with His grace, the unction of the HOLY SPIRIT, to sweeten the bitterness of repentance; when He makes it taste that *hidden manna*[1] which is promised to those who resist temptation and fight manfully against their enemies—it is then that all the harshness of penitence disappears, and pleasure is found in refusing pleasure for the love of GOD. Oh! didst thou but know the sweetness of repentance: would it be so much dreaded, so long deferred?

" That is surely pleasant toil whereby safety is attained."—*S. Cypr.*

Love of Money.

THE immoderate love—not the possession —of wealth is a sin. Our LORD does not reprove the rich, but the covetous. *The love of money*, saith S. Paul, *is the root of all evil.*[2] It first begets, and then nurses sin.

[1] Rev. ii. 17.   [2] 1 Tim. vi. 10.

What crimes the pursuit of riches, what crimes their possession causes! Rich and unprincipled men can do what they like, and what limit is there to *the desire of the wicked ?*[1] He that is over-eager in the pursuit of wealth will soon be lukewarm in GOD's service. He makes gold his idol, and the object of his love and worship, and in it places all his trust. He may not admit this, but his actions prove it.

Other lusts grow weak with advancing years, this one gains strength; others are calmed when their object is attained, this is stimulated. It is like a raging fire which burns the more fiercely the more it is fed with fuel. A covetous man is unjust, violent, hard, suspicious, knavish, faithless, without law, without affection. He ignores the claims of relations, of friends, of GOD. Self-interest is his only god : to it he sacrifices honour, conscience, salvation, everything.

" Hungering after wealth a man loses faith ; scraping together gold he squanders grace."—*S. Ambr.*

[1] Psalm cxl. 8.

The Blindness of Impurity.

DARKNESS is the most ordinary and disastrous consequence of the sin of impurity. It is the deadly plague with which GOD smites the unchaste. Their lawless lusts become their punishment. Having yielded themselves to inordinate desires, GOD yields them to uncleanness and the wanderings of a blinded spirit by which they are incited to the most shameful offences. As soon as a man becomes unchaste, he begins to lose his reason; what little light remains is gradually smothered and extinguished. By purity a man is like unto an angel; by its loss he sinks to the level of a brute.

Impurity deprives a man of the light of grace as well as of that of reason. Grace cannot *dwell in the body that is subject to sin.*[1] Sooner might *light* have *communion with darkness* than the purity of grace with the impurity of the wicked. *The natural man*, saith S. Paul, *receiveth not the things of the Spirit of God*;[2] there is in him an incapacity of conversion. Nothing, S. Augustine declares, is harder than to convert the unchaste. What

---

[1] Wisd. i. 4.   [2] 1 Cor. ii. 14.

Saint was more illuminated than David? and yet, through adultery, he became so blinded as to live for months without reflecting on his sin, and needed a prophet to open his eyes and bring him to repentance.

Once more, impurity extinguishes the light of faith. When it has reached a certain point it leaves men confirmed libertines and unbe-lievers. They regard it not as sin but as a necessity. Christian mortification and peni-tence is to them a dream, and the rule of chastity a tyrannical yoke which it is impos-sible to bear. From practice they go on to doctrine. Errors of conduct create errors of creed. Hell-fire is an inconvenient truth to a libertine; he doubts first, and then denies it. No one, according to S. Augustine, says *There is no God*,[1] but he whose interest it is there should be none. The cause of Solo-mon's idolatry was his worship of fleshly idols.

"The foul exhalations of carnal lust dark-ened my heart."—*S. Aug.*

[1] Psalm liii. 1.

Lukewarmness described.

WHAT is lukewarmness? It is a state *neither cold nor hot*,[1]—a mixture of good and evil. A lukewarm person will not commit deadly, but readily falls into little sins; he does not give way to violent ebullitions of temper, but he is bitter of speech, peevish, and impatient; though not a gross slanderer, he says ill-natured things; he leads a moral, but self-indulgent, useless life; without coveting his neighbour's things, he is too much attached to his own; he practises good works, but without zeal or purity of intention; comes often to the Sacrament, but without due preparation; he confesses his sins, but there is no amendment; frequent as his communions are, they do not increase his fervour; he makes long prayers, but inattentively and indevoutly. So then he does what is right, but not in the right way; he acts under the influence of passing influences, without fixed rule, and in a wrong spirit. To do what is right in this way is not to do it at all.

Once more, the lukewarm are patient as long as they are not called to suffer; meek,

[1] Rev. iii. 15.

H

provided they be not contradicted; humble, if men honour them; charitable, when they are put to no inconvenience. They would be saints without the virtues which make saintliness, or at least without the trouble of acquiring them. They would conquer their unruly appetites, provided they were not compelled to combat them. In fine, they would be saved, but without much trouble, and win *Heaven* quietly, without taking *it by force*.[1]

Does your own conduct not exhibit this dangerous combination of feelings? A little warmth reassures you, when it should make you tremble; for it is the very characteristic of the lukewarm, whom the LORD hath threatened to *spew out of* His *mouth*.[2]

" Remember, not the lukewarm, not the listless, but the ' violent take Heaven by force.' "—*S. Aug.*

Christ's Agony.

IT was not so much the cruelty as the futility of His sufferings that cost our SA-VIOUR the keenest pangs. Cruel as they were

[1] S. Matth. xi. 12.   [2] Rev. iii. 16.

they had seemed sweet could He have hoped to save the whole world. Those thorns, those nails, that cross, had ceased to torture, could He have hoped to touch thy heart, and ensure thy salvation. But the thought that while His Blood more than sufficed to ransom a million worlds, it would not soften the hardness of thy heart, or win thy love, or procure thy salvation,—ah! that was the *cup* which He prayed might *pass*[1] from Him.

If the prospect of His approaching torments filled our SAVIOUR's heart with anguish, much more did the thought of our sins, the burden of which He was shortly to bear, overpower Him. What violence He did His heart when He forced it to bear the sins of mankind! He hated sin as much as He loved the FATHER; and this same love, while inspiring a horror of sin, made Him bear, in order to destroy it! A single sin had been an unsupportable weight, and He finds Himself burdened with the sins of a world! Can we wonder if, GOD though He was, His strength failed? Sin—such was its hideousness—was about to make Him *a curse*,[2] *in Whom* His FATHER was *well-pleased*.[3] All His other sufferings had a limit; this alone.

[1] S. Matth. xxvi. 39.   [2] Gal. iii. 13.
[3] S. Matth. iii. 17.

had none. As the grievousness, as the multitude of our sins, as the hatred He bears them, as His love for us, is infinite, so also His anguish. He had before His eyes every sinner; not a sin escaped His notice, or rather, not a sin spared His sorrow-stricken heart. Thine were there with those of other men; that sin which seemed to thee so sweet, filled thy SAVIOUR's breast with unspeakable bitterness. If thou wouldest know its grievousness, see how it afflicts the heart of JESUS, instead of judging by the corrupt feelings of thine own. How exceeding great must His agony have been to wring from Him that plaintive cry, *My soul is exceeding sorrowful, unto death;* to cause Him to draw back *sore amazed,* and pray the FATHER to spare Him the *cup,*[1]—not of bodily sufferings, for He had eagerly desired them, but—of our sins which must be drunk to the dregs.

That the SON of GOD should die for men is a perfect miracle of love; but that He should die for His enemies is a still more marvellous and affecting truth. He Himself has declared that there can be no more convincing proof of love than the willingness to die for a friend. He however carries His devotion further, and dies for enemies. And

[1] S. Mark xiv. 33—35.

such enemies—vile, insolent, ungrateful men!
To avenge Himself, He had only to forget
them, and they had become nothingness;
only to will their punishment, and they had
been eternally miserable. Yet far from punishing them as they deserve, He waits for
them, bears with them, prevents them with
grace, offers them His love, and dies a most
shameful and cruel death to atone for sins
committed against Himself! Could GOD,
Almighty though He be, carry His love
further?

By redeeming us at such a price, He teaches
us to value as we should, GOD's glory, and
spare no pains to secure it. He brings home
the nature of sin and enables us to estimate
the magnitude of the disease by the greatness
of the remedy required; for, as S. Bernard
observes, "Our wounds must needs be very
dangerous, since only a GOD by His wounds
could heal them." Lastly, He makes us realize the greatness of His love in order that,
if the very ease with which He had created
us had furnished a pretext for ingratitude, all
He underwent to ransom us might positively
compel our love. Alas! if, in spite of all these
sufferings our love is still so weak, what
would it have been if He had never suffered?

"Had we not been loved as enemies, we had never become His friends."—*S. Bern.*

Christ left us an Example.

CHRIST suffered that He might give us an example. By suffering He has furnished us with a potent motive for patient endurance, and at the same time earned us assisting grace. The Eternal FATHER, pointing to His SON on Calvary, says to every Christian what He said unto Moses, Follow the *pattern which was showed thee on the Mount.*[1] You cannot be predestined if you are not a copy of that Divine Original. His Passion cannot profit unless you are fastened with Him on the Cross. But are you crucified while you lead a carnal self-indulgent life ?

What we must above all imitate in CHRIST's Passion is the spirit in which He sacrificed all to His FATHER's glory. Mankind—blind, stupid, and intoxicated with self-love—could not realize GOD's nature, what He deserved, and what His glory demanded of them. It needed that a GOD-man should offer to His

[1] Exodus xxv. 40.

FATHER'S glory a perfect life-long oblation, by sacrificing His own welfare, happiness, glory, life itself. Christian, there is thy *pattern*. A SAVIOUR has given it out of love to thee; all thy happiness and glory lie in self-sacrifice to GOD, because thou art made for Him; the loss of thine all, sacrificed to His glory, gains for thee an infinite reward, and in losing all thou regainest all because thou regainest GOD Himself.

"Let Him be firmly seated in your heart Who was fastened on the Cross for you."— *S. Aug.*

The Death-bed of Sinners.

WHAT a state shall the sinner's be in the hour of death,—what terror, what troubles, what a conflict of desires and emotions! Through life he has had little faith, at death he shall have much, only to trouble and torment him; through life he has indulged in unreasonable and presumptuous hopes, at death his despair shall be still more groundless; through life he might have loved GOD, and he would not, at death he shall desire, and not be able. He will curse the wealth, the pleasures, the creatures which he has preferred to GOD and his salvation, but he will not be weaned from them; confounded at the recollection of his sins, he will not repent; or if he does, it will only be a forced repentance such as shall make him miserable without making him penitent.

He will be tormented in the hour of death by the review of the past. He will remember the grace he has abused, and long to have it back, but with justice it shall be refused. The means of grace might easily have ensured his salvation, but he has neglected them; now their want renders his salvation impossible. He will be tormented by the thought of those sinful pleasures which, vain, light, brief, as they at the time seemed, are now drawing down upon him eternal punishment! All that he has hated during life will now be desired in vain; all that he has loved, will now prove a source of torment and despair. Alas, he will change his mind without changing his heart!

Still more cruelly is he tortured by the fear of what is coming. He sees that in a few hours he must pass from time into eternity, —an eternity of misery to those who lack grace. Far from feeling assured of grace, far from the Spirit bearing witness to his being a child of GOD and an inheritor of the kingdom of heaven, he has but too visible proofs before him of his reprobation in the multitude and magnitude of his offences, in the hardness of his heart, in his troubled conscience, in his distrust of GOD's mercy, in his despair of salvation. Thus he finds himself in a condition which is at once a frightful picture and foretaste of that hell into which he is soon to fall.

"As a punishment for neglecting GOD in life, the sinner neglects himself in death."— *S. Aug.*

Heaven.

THE SON of GOD would have us so strengthened by the contemplation of the bliss of heaven as to endure the pains and persecutions of the world, not with patience only, but with joy, yea, a joy akin to rapture. *Rejoice,* He says, *and be exceeding glad.*[1] *Great* must the *reward* be if we are told to rejoice at purchasing it at the price of so much suffering. It cost our SAVIOUR much to pur-

[1] S. Matth. v. 12.

chase Heaven for us, and we would have it cost us nothing! His heavy cross appeared light when He considered the end. Faith teaches us that the way of the Cross can alone bring us to that end—that it is the way opened for us by CHRIST, and yet we dread and avoid it! How can we hope to reach our *desired haven*[1] if we refuse to follow the only road which can bring us to it?

Heaven must be an abode of blessedness indeed since it is the grandest evidence of GOD's magnificence. He appears rich and bountiful in all His gifts, but here alone shall He appear magnificent. Earth, sea, and sky, the starry firmament, and all His marvellous works show forth the glory of the LORD, but in Heaven only shall His dazzling splendour be exhibited. In hell alone shall He punish, in Heaven alone shall He recompense, as befits the Majesty of GOD. The evils of this life are but drops compared with the coming deluge of GOD's wrath; present joys but drops of the torrent of delight in which the blessed shall hereafter bathe. If we taste so many sweets here in the place of banishment, what shall be the blessedness of our fatherland! Woe to us if we prefer this place of exile to our home!

[1] Psalm cvii. 30.

"When thou waxest faint, look to the reward."—*S. Aug.*

A bad Example.

A MERE spark has before now reduced whole cities to ashes. A smile, an immodest look, an ambiguous word, an undue exposure of the person, a bad example sometimes lights a fire in some innocent heart which can never again be extinguished. Fathers and mothers, who give a bad example to your children, what an account shall ye render unto GOD! Ye have given natural life to your children only to slay the life of their souls. Alas, what an account shall they who have used their influence amiss, have to give! Theirs are, as it were, original sins which go on multiplying with an unhappy fruitfulness. Seldom is it possible to arrest or repair such evils; and yet, because they might have been foreseen and avoided, their authors shall not be justified before GOD.

Alas! the great and influential, heads of families and employers of labour, are often, without knowing it, treasuring up wrath which shall burst upon them when they least expect it, owing to some dependent or child fallen into sin by their example or indulgence. The sin shall be laid to their account. Theirs is the fault, theirs the responsibility. Terrible thought! they can go on sinning in the person of another, when they have ceased to sin themselves. Is the weight of their own sins not sufficient without burdening themselves with the sins of others?

"Sins may be repented of, but the scandal remains."—*S. Bern.*

Aboid occasions of Sin.

OCCASIONS of sin, sought or unsought, are to be feared. The greatest saints have ever dreaded them, whether caused by chance, or necessity, or the malice of the demon; nor did they think it unworthy of their Christian courage to turn pale at the sight of a danger which imperilled their salvation. Most of all are occasions to be feared when deliberately courted. The saintly Psalmist fell because he allowed his eyes to fasten on a dangerous object which presented itself to them unsought, unawares, and at a distance. How much more reason then have the young, with passions as strong as their principles are weak, with impressionable and corrupted hearts, with excitable and unbridled senses, to fear the results, if they deliberately place themselves in the way of objects all the more dangerous in proportion as their influence is felt? What can be expected in their case but a fatal fall?

A man seeks an occasion of sin only because it affords him pleasure; the pleasure is due to the attracting presence of certain objects; the greater their influence, the more must they sway his heart and passions, and the feebler must his resistance be. Is he not certain then to be overcome by a temptation which he has apparently sought out for the sole purpose of being vanquished? If he could not resist the inclination to place himself in the way of temptation, how shall he find strength to resist when sin solicits him with her manifold attractions? If free from all external pressure he could not stand firm on the edge of the precipice, how shall he arrest his fall when dragged downwards by the violence of his passions, and fascinated by their object?

Fly we then the occasions of sin if we would avoid sin. Let us not help our foes by

I

throwing ourselves in their way. They are strong enough already; alone they are more than a match for us. Why strengthen their hands? why furnish them with weapons against us? The greatest saints, with all their strength and courage, have deemed flight their safest course, fear and watchfulness their best allies. Christian heroes have been seen to quail at the sight of dangers in which they had become involved through charity and zeal. And yet we, presumptuous as we are weak, feel no alarm amid temptations into which our passions and lusts have precipitated us! In what can such groundless confidence issue but in disastrous falls?

"Joseph's weapon of defence was flight."
—*S. Ambr.*

Frequent Communions.

WE ought to communicate frequently since JESUS invites us to do so. *Come unto Me*, He says, *all ye that labour and are heavy laden, and I will give you rest.*[1] Our frailties are no obstacles provided they are

[1] S. Matth. xi. 28.

displeasing to us. He invites the sick, the blind, and the halt to His Supper in order to show that none are shut out because they are not in perfect health. By making use of food in the institution of this Sacrament, He signifies that the soul can no more dispense with spiritual, than the body with material food. He gives us His Body under the species of bread, because bread is our common food; other articles of diet we often change, but we never change this. He promises great blessings to those who approach, He threatens with great evils those who turn their backs upon this Sacrament. The power of the Priest to dispense is as unlimited as that of the faithful to approach It.

We ought to communicate frequently because the Church urges us to do so. The Fathers are her interpreters, and they enjoin this duty with one voice. Why, says S. Ambrose, not receive daily that which can daily profit you? All who are present at the Holy Mysteries are earnestly exhorted to communicate. Such was the teaching she gave to the early Christians, and in proportion as her sons and daughters have carried out this holy practice, in so far have they proved saints indeed. How inconsistent is man! GOD forbids him, on pain of death, *to*

eat of the tree of the knowledge of good and evil,[1]
and he *eats;* GOD commands him, on pain
of death, to *eat*[2] of *the Bread of Life,* and he
eats not! In this Sacrament we receive not
merely grace, but the Source and Author of
grace, even the LORD Himself, Who fills us
with abundant outpourings of spiritual gifts,
applies to each the price of His Blood, the
virtue of His merits, and filling us with His
Spirit unites us to Himself.

"There is no presumption in communicating often, but there is in coming but once
unworthily."—*S. Chrys.*

𝔘nforgiving, unforgiven.

HE who will not forgive others, must despair of being forgiven himself. He
alone who needs not GOD's pardon, can
avenge himself with impunity. But where is
that man? As sinners we have no other resource than GOD's mercy,—can we expect it
if we show none to others? *Forgive, and ye
shall be forgiven,*[3]—these are our SAVIOUR's

---

[1] Gen. ii. 17.   [2] S. Matth. xxvi. 26.
[3] S. Luke vi. 37.

terms. I can only enter Heaven through mercy's gate; I close it upon myself when I refuse it to my brother. Can my bitterest enemy do me a worse turn?

A vindictive person renders nugatory the most effectual means of grace; he excommunicates himself. No more prayers, no more sacraments, no more sacrifices for him; the most salutary remedies become baneful. He cannot pray without self-condemnation. His prayer becomes a horrible imprecation; he opens his lips only to condemn himself: what a prayer! He asks GOD not to pardon him, but to hate him, to destroy him, to damn him! Must not the desire of vengeance blind a man terribly to reduce him to such a position? It is not mere passion, it is infatuation, it is madness!

"He who denies pardon to another, denies it to himself."—*S. Leo.*

Impediments to Self-knowledge.

NOTHING is more important than self-knowledge. It is the foundation of humility. Men are proud simply because they lack self-knowledge.   As well know nothing, as know everything and not know oneself. To what purpose the knowledge of the laws of the universe if we know not what is passing in ourselves ?   We are not entrusted with the government of the universe, but of our own hearts: we must watch and regulate their movements.   Besides, self-knowledge is a great step to the knowledge of GOD.   We cannot know ourselves without perceiving our own nothingness, misery, and dependence on Him, and learning the being, fulness, and universal sovereignty of GOD, which we cannot escape for a single moment.

Unhappily, far from diligent self-inspection, we make ignorance of ourselves our special aim.   Carelessness has much to do with this : self-examination is troublesome, so we put it aside : but pride is the principal cause.   Self-knowledge humiliates : it brings to light so many imperfections and failings.   Such a discovery offends our self-esteem, it must be avoided.   Better retain self-complacency by keeping our eyes shut, than be humiliated by self-knowledge.

Self-love, too, is a common cause of this state of ignorance.   We hug our vices and foibles, our most inordinate affections maintain their hold, we are in no hurry to part with them. Now it would be difficult, when once self-examination had laid bare all the unruly motions of our hearts, not to realize their dreadful character, fear their results, and see the necessity of curing them. We should need courage to take such a step, we should have to do ourselves great and constant violence. It is here that pride, self-love, and sloth stand in the way. How are the frivolous and faint-hearted to screw up their courage to the task?

"Let me know myself, let me know Thee."—*S. Aug.*

Ineffectual Prayer.

HOW comes it that, although CHRIST has attributed such unfailing efficacy to prayer made in His Name, it is for the most part so ineffectual? Because we pray in a state of sin. A sinner who longs not for a change of heart, cannot use the prayer CHRIST taught, without self-contradiction and self-condemnation. How pray, *Hallowed be Thy Name*,[1] while he wilfully unhallows it? How, *Thy kingdom come*, while he rebels against GOD,

[1] S. Matth. vi. 9.

and enthrones sin in his heart? How, *Thy will be done*, while breaking His commandments? How, ask for *daily bread* only to eat It[1] unworthily? How say, *forgive*, only to fall into fresh *trespasses?* How, petition Him to *deliver from evil*, while resolutely abiding in sin? What a mass of inconsistencies; what ample grounds for condemnation!

Again, prayer miscarries, because you ask for something wrong. You ask for success in some unrighteous design—is it not a fresh sin to ask GOD to aid and abet what is wrong? You ask for health or the good things of this life, and He foresees that the immoderate love or abuse of them would prove an obstacle to your salvation, a curse rather than a blessing; you want happiness, and He knows it would prove to you a source of sin and thus of sorrow—are your prayers then not best answered when denied? Ah, LORD, deny me all that would prove an obstacle to my salvation; this is the answer I would have.

Once more, prayer is ineffectual because it is not offered in a proper spirit. *Ye ask*, says S. James, *and receive not, because ye ask amiss.*[2]

---

[1] A common interpretation of the Fathers, in harmony with our LORD's words in the same chapter (verse 33) and including the lower sense.

[2] S. James iv. 3.

Your prayer wants the conditions needed to render it effectual. You pray indevoutly, inattentively: how expect GOD to hear when you do not hear yourself? You pray irreverently, and let your very *prayer become sin* :[1] shall you be heard while offending Him? You pray without that lively faith which our SAVIOUR has always made an indispensable condition—He said not, *Ask, and ye shall receive,*[2] but, *Ask believing,* and *ye shall receive.*[3] Lastly, you wax faint and weary, whereas the efficacy of prayer usually depends on perseverance. What wonder that your prayers are not answered while they lack all these conditions ?

" A petition is not offered in our SAVIOUR's name which is hurtful to our salvation."—*S. Aug.*

On following Christ.

THOU art a Christian in name, but art thou one in deed ? Thou bearest the sign, livest thou the life it signifies ? Thinkest thou that a little water sprinkled in Baptism made thee a perfect Christian ? That indeed is necessary, but it is not enough. A Chris-

---

[1] Ps. cix. 7. [2] S. John xvi. 24. [3] S. Matth. xxi. 22.

tian takes CHRIST for his example and the Gospel for his rule of conduct, tries to become a lively copy of the Divine Original, so as to seem to reflect CHRIST in every feature, and to live His life.   Art thou then a Christian? CHRIST was humble, thou art vain and proud; He shrank from honours, thou seekest them eagerly; He was gentle and meek, thou canst bear nothing; He forgave the heaviest wrongs, thou not the lightest; He loved His very murderers, thou not even thy brethren; He embraced a life of poverty, thou covetest the world's goods; His was a painful, self-denying life, thine is easy and self-indulgent; He denied Himself the most innocent pleasures, thou allowest thyself the most dangerous and perchance, licentious; He was *obedient unto death, even the death of the Cross*,[1] thou wilt not obey in the easiest matters; He sought His own pleasure in nothing, thou in everything. Alas! the death of CHRIST will avail thee nothing if His life hath not been thy rule.   His merits will not profit if thou hast not profited by His example.   He cannot be thy SAVIOUR if He has not been thy Pattern.

"I am no Christian unless I follow CHRIST." —*S. Bern.*

[1] Phil. ii. 8.

Christ's hidden life.

WHO can understand the conduct of CHRIST in His hidden life? He comes to effect the conversion of the world, and He dwells for thirty years in a workshop, leading an obscure and apparently useless life! Why imprison such ardent zeal in a shop? Why hide such a burning and a shining light under a bushel? Why bury such marvellous talents? Why not traverse the world to instruct it by His teaching, to edify it by His example, to astonish it by His miracles, and to convert it by the influence of His holiness and the power of His words? Why in a word, spend thirty years in doing nothing when He might have been doing such great things for the glory of GOD? How impenetrable these mysteries appear; how marvellous when penetrated!

How much was CHRIST doing in His hidden life while He seemed to be doing nothing! When doing the will of His FATHER, was He doing nothing? When teaching us to understand that to remain passive in obedience to GOD's command is better than to do the greatest actions against it, was He doing nothing? When His hidden life was furnishing us with so powerful a remedy against pride and the desire of being seen, was He doing nothing? When He converted that shop into a school, and by His noble lessons, made known the value, inspired the esteem, and taught the practice of humility, was He doing nothing?

How His hidden life condemns your pride and eagerness to be known and seen of men.[1] Zeal throws you into some important movement; you want to do great things, to attract notice by praiseworthy acts; to take part in everything. Alas! it is to be feared that in so doing, you do nothing: for to do much, and not do it for GOD's sake, is to do nothing. Is it not vanity that sends you abroad? is not self-love the mainspring, and a desire of show, of popularity, of praise, the cause of your addiction to good works? are you not all the time neglecting the obscure duties of common life simply because they attract no notice?

"Standing still is often the best service."[2] —*S. Aug.*

[1] S. Matth. vi. 5.
[2] Nostrum otium magnum negotium est.

Rules of neighbourly Love.

THE first rule of charity is to love our neighbour as ourselves. We love ourselves tenderly ; we feel the least evil which affects ourselves, and even magnify it till it appears great ; we conceal from ourselves our faults, or at least represent them as light ones. We should do this in the case of our neighbour also.

Secondly, we must love our neighbour as we would in turn be loved. This is CHRIST's own rule : *As ye would that men should do to you, do ye also to them likewise.*[1] O divine rule of all righteousness ! We have but to take self-love, perverted as it is, for our rule ; it will make us just to others. Let each ask himself, Should I like to be used in this way, harshly treated, spoken to contemptuously, ordered about imperiously, maliciously slandered, laughed and sneered at ; to have my lightest faults caught hold of and exaggerated, my most innocent acts misconstrued, my purest intentions cruelly misinterpreted, my conduct condemned on the faintest pretext, no allowance made for my infirmities, no patience ex-

[1] S. Luke vi. 31.

K

ercised towards my faults ?　Should I not like to be treated in the very opposite way ?　Why, then, not myself observe the same rule with my neighbours ?

Thirdly, we must love others as CHRIST has loved us.　He loved us when we were without merit, when we were His enemies. He loved us disinterestedly in spite of our wretchedness and vileness.　He loved us to the sacrifice of happiness, peace, glory, life.

"Blessed is he who loves Thee, a friend in Thee, a foe for Thee."—*S. Aug.*

Conformity to God's Will.

THE lowest degree of conformity to the will of GOD, consists in accepting it with considerable repugnance, but yet unresistingly.　We do not allow ourselves to murmur, but plaints at times escape us ; we would not oppose His will, but we should like it to jump with our own, so that we pray with more eagerness and anxiety than true fervour ; we would not use wicked means to attain our ends, but possibly we might stoop to very questionable ones ; there is no open rebellion, but a lurking spirit of discontent. This is a very imperfect state, and yet it is quite possible that you have not yet reached it.

The next degree consists in submitting to God's will. Repugnance there may be, but it is fought against ; sadness is tempered with resignation ; far from murmuring we do not even utter complaints, or if they do escape us through natural weakness, our hearts instantly recall and condemn them ; the earliest uprisings of a rebellious spirit are promptly stifled, and a renewal made of the sacrifice of the will to God.

The highest degree consists in loving God's will even when it seems harshest. Not to love His will, is not to love God. His will is righteous and holy ; we must be unrighteous and wicked if we do not love it. We naturally love what is good ; can anything but good proceed from a will which is infinitely good ? If the greatest evils, when willed by God, change their nature and become blessings, we ought to accept them not with resignation merely, but with joy. A heart when thus disposed becomes a positive paradise, and its possessor blessed indeed.

" In adversity thank God, and in prosperity confess thine unworthiness."—*Eucher.*

God's Presence.

GOD sees me,—solemn thought for him that comprehends it! How it should curb our passions, moderate our desires, prevent our sins, sustain our courage, animate our zeal, in short, rule our conduct! He is ever thinking of me, ever mindful of me, ever present with me; while I, alas! scarcely ever am mindful or think of Him. With what respect and modesty should I behave in His presence! The seraphim prostrate themselves before His throne, and I, a worm, feel no awe! The most insolent of men dare not insult the majesty of kings, and I am not held back by the Majesty of GOD! Dare I, in His sight who cannot look upon iniquity commit an action which I dare not commit before a fellow-man? dare I sin before Him Who infinitely abhors sin, and has but to will to destroy the sinner?

GOD sees me,—He will crown with infinite blessedness the least good action, the faintest good desire; He penetrates the depths of my heart, discerns all its stirrings, traces all its motives, tests the purity of its intentions. He sees me when I am most strongly tempted, cheers me in the combat, helps me to stand firm, and holds out a crown to urge me on to victory.

He sees me in affliction,—all I suffer, and how I suffer; He is not insensible to my troubles, and takes account of my patience; is ready when I seek Him, either to deliver, if it be for His glory and my salvation, or else to strengthen me lest I give way. *Why art thou cast down, O my soul?*[1] GOD seeth all thy sorrows, compassionates thy secret sighs, anticipates thy wants, hears thy prayers. What then canst thou want, unless thou wantest trust in GOD?

" Angels and the Angels' GOD witness thy conflict with the devil."—*Ephrem.*

The Fruits of the Spirit.

FIRST, the descent of the HOLY GHOST wrought in the hearts of the Apostles a sincere and ardent charity. It alone can impart the gift of love, so that we must receive It before we can love. It came in the likeness of fire, because its mission was to kindle in every heart that Divine love which JESUS

[1] Psalm xlii. 5.

had promised. No sooner had the Apostles received It, than they were fired with love, and went through the world kindling it in the coldest hearts. Alas! does not the coldness of your heart show that you have not suffered it to be warmed by this Divine flame? is it not smothered by some impure fire burning within?

Next, the HOLY GHOST produced in the Apostles such an ardent zeal for the glory of CHRIST, as to drive them into every land for the purpose of making Him known and publishing His greatness. Twelve fishermen, without repute, without education, or eloquence, or talent, but armed with the HOLY SPIRIT, were seen traversing the world, proclaiming their Master's glory, and compelling philosophers and sages, the world's great ones, kings and emperors to believe that a crucified criminal was GOD!

Once more, the HOLY SPIRIT produced in the Apostles marvellous courage amid the greatest perils, and heroic constancy under the direst sufferings. These very disciples, before so faint-hearted and cowardly as to forsake their Master, while the bravest and chief of them, frightened by a woman's voice, denied Him,—on receiving the Spirit, became forthwith brave as lions, freely dared the utmost perils, bearded tyrants, laughed at torture, preached CHRIST on the scaffold, suffered death with constancy and joy, and sealed with their blood a life-long witness to their LORD's Divinity! Does your dread of proclaiming yourself on His side, and setting at nought the world's opinion, not prove that you still want that strength which is at once the fruit and evidence of the Spirit's presence in the heart?

"Their courage in preaching exceeds their cowardice in hiding."—*S. Bern.*

The Measure of Grace.

THERE is a measure of grace. When much has been vouchsafed, and exhausted, we cannot hope for more. *Unto every one of us*, saith the Apostle, *is given grace according to the measure of the gift of Christ.*[1] GOD in His infinite wisdom weighs and measures everything. If there falls not a leaf to the ground except He wills it, can we suppose that He abandons the distribution of His grace to chance?

[1] Ephes. iv. 7.

There is also a measure of sin. However much the wrath of GOD is kindled against the inhabitants of Sodom, He says that He cannot yet punish them, because the measure of their sins is not yet filled. He pardons the city of Damascus three transgressions, but He declares that the fourth shall fill up the measure of their iniquities and of His long-suffering. The measure of sin is filled to the brim, when the measure of grace is spent. S. Paul calls the first a *treasure of wrath* ; the other, *the riches of His goodness.*[1] Does your waste of so much grace not make you fear lest your measure become exhausted, lest the grace you are now despising be all that shall be vouchsafed ?

The measure is usually filled up by the abuse of great, special grace. The arm of GOD is stretched out to strike sinners, when it has been in vain stretched out to bless ; the neglect of an abundance of grace is followed by abandonment. To whom was more grace vouchsafed than to Saul, when GOD chose him to be the first ruler of His people ? But he was untrue to it, and therefore he was abandoned by GOD both in life and death. How much grace was lavished upon Jerusalem during CHRIST's sojourn there ! It was

[1] Rom. ii. 4, 5.

the time of her visitation which, as He Himself declared, she knew not ; and how terrible were the results ! And thine own hardness of heart, after the voice of grace has urged thee so often to repent,—is it not a righteous judgment caused by thy neglect of it ?

" GOD Himself witnesseth that there is a limit and measure of sins."—*S. Aug.*

Salvation a difficult work.

TO *work out our salvation*[1] is a hard task. Why disguise a truth which our SAVIOUR has so plainly declared ? He does not humour us on this point. It is that *treasure hid in a field,*[2] that *pearl of great price,*[3] acquired at the cost of all besides, that *narrow way* along which few have the courage to pass, that *strait gate*[4] by which it is so hard to enter. Could the SAVIOUR have made this truth more evident than He has by so many parables and similitudes ?

And in truth how many obstacles stand in the way, how many foes beset our path !

[1] Phil. ii. 12.
[2] S. Matth. xiii. 44.
[3] S. Matth. xiii. 46.
[4] S. Matth. vii. 13.

Concupiscence has to be tamed, violent passions to be moderated, unruly senses to be mortified, inveterate habits to be rooted out, objects pleasant as they are fatal to be shunned, dangerous occasions to be avoided, strong ties to be broken. What firmness, what strength, what courage is needed to combat the enemies which beset our path—the Flesh, a traitor in the citadel, to be feared the more the less we fear it, by how much flattered, by so much dangerous—the World with its corrupt maxims, its enticing promises, its ensnaring examples —the Demon, that crafty, watchful, malignant foe, whose first concern is our perdition, while our salvation is our last!

Heaven can only be won by mighty conflicts and ceaseless watching. There is a crown, but it can only be earned by them that conquer in the fight. We must *not faint*, but *resist unto blood, striving against sin.*[1] Great efforts are required, and we act like cowards; constant vigilance, and we slumber; we are summoned to the fight, and we fly; natural inclinations need to be mortified, and we yield to them without a struggle! How reconcile all this with a sincere wish to be saved? What, wish to be saved and do the very opposite of what is required! If we had

[1] Heb. xii. 4.

been placed on earth to work out our perdition instead of our salvation, would our conduct not be just what it is ?

" Your advancement shall be proportionate to the violence you do yourself."—*De Imit. Christi.*

Hardness of Heart.

GOD and man contribute towards the hardening of the heart. Man begins the work, GOD finishes it. Man by committing sin, GOD by punishing it; man by resisting the light of grace, GOD by withdrawing it. Man is unrighteous and wicked in hardening himself, GOD is holy and just in hardening the sinner. Blindness of spirit is the cause, hardness of heart the penalty. At other times GOD chastises as a FATHER, but here He punishes as an enemy. There men are often made penitents, here, only reprobates. A hardened heart is the beginning of reprobation—it is blinded, not enlightened by the light; GOD's strokes as they fall with an ever-increasing weight produce rebellion instead of submission; His plagues overwhelm instead of humbling; His miracles confound without converting. He displays His power and greatness towards a hardened sinner, in judgment, not in mercy. He showed forth His might not less in punishing Pharaoh than in converting Nebuchadnezzar.

Would you know the marks of a hard heart? Listen to S. Bernard: That heart is hard which contrition breaks not, devotion softens not, prayer touches not; which yields not to GOD's threats, but hardens under His strokes; which is ungrateful to Him for favours, and corresponds not to grace; which blushes not for the most shameful things, fears not the greatest dangers, is without natural affection, or fear of GOD, oblivious of the past, careless about the present, blind to the future, forgetful of its duties, and heedless of its end.

"Wouldst thou know a hard heart? Unless thou fearest greatly, thine is one."— *S. Bern.*

Fear of the World's Opinion.

MUCH faith is needed to believe in a crucified GOD, but when we are convinced that He is GOD, why be ashamed to serve and do homage to Him before the world? You acknowledge and boast that CHRIST is your Master, and yet you are ashamed to be His servant and disciple; you profess to be a Christian, and you blush to appear a good one; you are proud of the name, and you shrink from proving your right to bear it! What inconsistency to believe in JESUS, and be ashamed of His Gospel; esteem His Law, and blush to practise it; profess His doctrine, and shrink from following His example; believe as a Christian, and live as a heathen! This is to *hold the truth in unrighteousness*,[1] to sin against the HOLY SPIRIT, to apostatise in heart.

It was fear of man's judgment that caused the death of the SON of GOD. Convinced of His innocence and of their wickedness, Pilate did not yield to the clamorous outcries of the Jews until they threatened him with the Emperor's anger. Fear of the Cæsar's displeasure made him yield. Alas, in how many hearts has the fear of the world's opinion caused CHRIST to die—in how many has it hindered His birth! We fear what fools may say of us—we do not fear hell. Are we not fools ourselves to fear the verdict of fools? is their contempt and blame not true praise?

[1] Rom. i. 18.

L

"Men blush to deny CHRIST, and they blush not to deny His teaching."—*S. Aug.*

Symptoms of Lukewarmness.

THE immediate result and first symptom of lukewarmness is the Readiness with which we omit our devotional exercises, our prayers, readings, and communions. The least difficulty turns us aside; the least pleasure is a sufficiently strong pretext for dispensing with them; our duty to GOD holds the last place, and we perform it when we feel inclined and have nothing better to do. A fervent spirit on the other hand gives GOD the highest place, and the claims of religion the earliest attention; the strongest reasons for setting them aside appear weak; nothing is allowed to stand in their way except sheer inability or some call of mercy; GOD is never forsaken unless it be for GOD. How often we forsake GOD for the world's trifles? Would we leave a King's company for that of a servant? and is GOD not great enough to be treated with the same respect?

A second symptom is Carelessness in the discharge of religious exercises—intended to honour they only dishonour Him. Prayer—irreverent, inattentive, indevout, ineffectual—becomes *sin*,[1] as saith the Psalmist, and GOD is provoked by the very act which is intended to appease Him. Confession is made without previous self-examination, without contrition, without steadfast resolution of amendment. The Holy Communion is received without holy dispositions, without fervour, without that living faith needed to profit by It, without that spiritual appetite which shows a hungering after the Divine Food and a right state of heart.

Another symptom is the habit of doing everything in an unreflecting, aimless way. Lukewarm persons act capriciously, under the influence of passion, through habit, out of regard to public opinion, or at the prompting of self-love. If they would only sound their hearts and candidly examine their actions, they would find scarcely anything done purely and simply for GOD'S sake ; and vanity, the gratification of the senses, self-seeking, and self-satisfaction, nearly always holding the chief place. Alas ! what shall be the astonishment of the lukewarm to find that after labouring much they have wrought nothing,

[1] Ps. cix. 7.

because actions which have not God for their end, count for nothing.

Another symptom is Negligence in acquiring virtues, overcoming failings, and practising good works. These are the three principal duties of Christians, but the pitiful inutility of their lives shows how much the lukewarm neglect them.

One more symptom of lukewarmness is a Disregard of Trifles—of petty duties, of little sins, of unimportant rules. People forget that nothing which displeases God can be a trifle; that Christ Himself has said, *He that is faithful in that which is least, is faithful also in much* ;[1] and that the discharge of numberless petty duties constitutes perfection.

"Better not be a believer at all than be a careless one."—*S. Ambr.*

Reverence in Church.

CHURCHES are God's temples whither man comes to pay homage to Him : how reverently then should we demean ourselves in them ! The Cherubim—those

[1] S. Luke xvi. 10.

spirits of spotless purity—cover their faces with their wings while prostrating themselves in lowliest reverence before His awful Majesty: how greatly then should we—worms and sinners—fear and tremble! The superstitious awe shown by the heathen in their temples condemns us, and yet they are only worshipping idols. To judge by their reverence, one would say that their idols are gods; to judge by our irreverence, that our GOD is an idol. If GOD *smote more than fifty thousand men of Bethshemesh because they had looked into the ark of the Lord,*[1] shall He not heavily punish those who profane His sanctuaries? How terribly incensed did our LORD, at all times so meek and gentle, show Himself against the profaners of the temple![2]

You come to church to adore GOD, and you insult Him by your irreverence; you come to appease His wrath, and you arouse it by your profanity; you come with a full knowledge of your misery to ask Him to supply your needs, and you exhibit the tokens of insolent pride; at the very moment that you are asking for grace, you are insulting His Divine Majesty, thus turning prayer— the highest religious act—into a sin and an abomination. Distraction, though so sinful

---

[1] 1 Sam. vi. 19.   [2] S. Matth. xxi. 12.

at such a time, is the least culpable defect in
your prayers. Dare you address Him in a
manner and posture in which you would not
dare address an earthly potentate? Is He
less worthy of respect than a mere worm?

Our chancels represent Calvary. With
what sentiments of humility, reverence, and
contrition should we enter them! Would
you have joined your SAVIOUR's enemies to
insult, and His executioners to torment Him?
And do you not, by your irreverence at the
Eucharist, renew the shame of His Passion,
which is therein commemorated?

"Behold the Heaven of heavens cannot
contain Thee, and Thou sayest, Come unto
Me."—*De Imit. Christi.*

Humility a Requisite.

YOU shall meet with the patient, charitable, liberal, chaste, temperate, and
meek, but where shall you find the really
humble? And yet that man is not a real
Christian who is not humble, and a real
Christian only can be humble. The ancient
philosophers who have so eloquently enlarged

on other virtues had not even a name for this one.

We can no more be saved without humility than without Baptism. CHRIST hath said, *Except a man be born again of water and the Spirit, he cannot enter into the kingdom of God.*[1] He has also said, *Except ye become as little children, ye cannot enter into the kingdom of God.*[2] Why then do we live as though we believed the one saying and not the other? The Gospel teaches us that there is no salvation without conformity to JESUS, and that we cannot have this conformity without humility. Is not our pride then a token of reprobation?

Humility is a virtue which belongs to all sorts and conditions of men. It is obligatory on the great as well as small. Mean folk are often humiliated without being made humble, while the great seek to be made humble without being humiliated. The latter must humble themselves beneath the mighty Hand of GOD, and recognize their absolute dependence upon Him; they must consider that all their power comes from Him, and that it must be used in His service, and that their meanest dependents may one day, through humility, occupy a far higher place than themselves.

[1] S. John iii. 5. [2] S. Matth. xviii. 3.

They must never forget how opposed theirs is to the mean and humble estate of their GOD, and that it must therefore be a great hindrance to conformity to Him, and a serious obstacle to their salvation.

"Humble thyself as thou wilt, thou shalt never be so humble as CHRIST."—*S. Jerome.*

The Necessity of Mortification.

WE cannot be saved without being Christians, or be Christians without mortifying our senses and inordinate affections. Baptism, according to S. Paul, represents to us the death and burial of CHRIST, binding us thenceforth to die to ourselves and sin, and to live unto Him. Hence this sacrament of life is a sacrament of death : it is at once our cradle and our tomb.[1] Living the life of grace, we are henceforth called to die to the motions of a sensual life and a corrupt nature. What else did all those baptismal ceremonies mean ? what those solemn renunciations pronounced on our behalf by those who held us

---

[1] Rom. vi. 1—11.

at the font, and which we subsequently confirmed as soon as we were old enough to comprehend the obligations incurred? Did you not bind yourself to a life of perpetual mortification? did you not bind yourself at the foot of the altar, before heaven and earth, to renounce the world and its pomps, the flesh and its pleasures, the devil and his works? Was it all an empty ceremony, which imposed no obligations whatever? It was a promise before GOD, more binding than any other vow soever.

We submit willingly to the annoyances and mortifications which our interests and passions entail: to satisfy them no price seems too great: but how few submit to those acts of self-denial which as Christians they are required to practise! How few, even among religious people, set themselves to the task of thoroughly rooting out a dominant sin! And yet this alone can be called true devotion, because it alone comprises the essential obligations of Christianity. All devotion that falls short of this is a mere delusion.

" Conquer thyself, and thou hast conquered the world."—*S. Aug.*

𝔓𝔲𝔯𝔦𝔱𝔶 𝔬𝔣 𝔍𝔫𝔱𝔢𝔫𝔱𝔦𝔬𝔫.

THE Apostle says, *Whether ye eat or drink,
or whatsoever ye do, do all to the glory of
God.*[1]   We belong to GOD on so many
grounds that everything that is in us should be
dedicated to Him.   We are His by creation,
by redemption, by regeneration.   All we have
comes from Him : all should therefore be de-
voted to Him.   He helps us in all our acts :
ought not then all our acts to harmonize with
His intentions ?

Sheer self-interest should lead us to refer all
our actions to GOD.   Good works thus become
better, and the most indifferent, good.   The
meanest action is thus ennobled, while it secures for us the indwelling presence of GOD,
and a higher degree of eternal glory.   Purity
of intention is a kind of spiritual alchemy
whereby that which is of least value is converted into gold.

What a consolation, to be able to arrive at
a high degree of perfection, not by doing anything extraordinary, but simply by referring all
we do to GOD ; to feel that He will reckon
up our poorest and most indifferent acts and

[1] 1 Cor. x. 31.

give an eternity of glory as their reward! What despair, on the other hand, shall we feel in the hour of death, on seeing that, through lack of a single intention, we have toiled much and gained nothing, *sown the wind* of empty, earthly motives, and *reaped the whirlwind.*[1]

" He doeth much that loveth much."—*De Imit. Christi.*

Union with Jesus in the Eucharist.

THE tenderness of the love of JESUS is shown in His desire and endeavour to unite Himself with us in the Eucharist in a union the most perfect, the most admirable, and the most inconceivable. What is said of the nature of GOD, may be said of the nature of this union, that it is easier to define what it is not than what it is, and that it can be believed and felt but not conceived or expressed. The Fathers compare it to that of fire with red-hot iron. Our LORD compares it to that of food taken into the body, the most intimate of all unions, because the former becomes one with the latter. His words are, *He that eateth*

---

[1] Hos. viii. 7.

My Flesh, and drinketh My Blood, dwelleth in Me and I in him.[1] It seems impossible to use stronger language, and yet He goes still further, comparing our oneness with Him in the Communion to His Oneness with the FATHER in the Trinity : *As I live by the Father, so he that eateth Me, even he shall live by Me.*[2] We, then, ought in our turn to show our love by our efforts to unite ourselves with Him by a lively faith, an ardent charity, and a perfect conformity of heart and spirit. This must be the result, yea, the infallible result, of a worthy reception. -How comes it then that it is so often wanting? Because we place obstacles in the way. Two things cannot be united so long as the least thing comes between them. Our sins, our passions, our ties, come between Him and us.

Help me, SAVIOUR, to overcome these obstacles : for how shameful to Thee as to me, that Thy power should be forced to yield to my obstinacy. Strip and bare my heart of all that hinders the union I desire with Thee. Stripped of them all I shall be rich if I possess Thee.

" What better gift than Himself could even He bestow ?"—*S. Bern.*

[1] S. John vi. 56.　　　　[2] S. John vi. 57.

The Peril of Declension.

IF you relapse so often into sin, have you no fear of losing the power of raising yourself again? Falls always enfeeble, much more do relapses enfeeble, and increase the difficulty of rising. He who is in a state of grace is united to GOD. Through a fall he is separated from GOD by an immeasurable interval, and gravitates towards hell. To recover himself he must make the most strenuous efforts; to be able to make them he must receive abundant grace. But does he who has so often lapsed and abused grace deserve to receive an extraordinary measure of it from GOD? Would his hopes of it not rest on a very precarious foundation? Far from their being well-grounded, he has every reason to despair of obtaining further supplies of grace because of the aggravating circumstances under which he has fallen. First, he has shown black ingratitude: he has received that precious gift of grace, which is the price of the Blood of a GOD-man, giving him an incontestable claim to the possession of GOD; he received this when he had no personal merit, when he was dead in sin, and yet he has valued it so little

M

as to be indifferent to its loss! Secondly, after
seeking pardon and grace with many tokens of
sorrow and penitence, he has despised them
when once more vouchsafed, thus insolently
making GOD's patience a motive and occasion
of sinning!

To ingratitude and contempt a backslider
adds perfidy.   After protestations so often re-
iterated and sealed, so to speak, with the Body
and Blood of CHRIST, he perfidiously forgets
and violates all his vows on the most trivial
grounds, under the lightest pressure, to please
some   miserable   creature,   to   satisfy   some
shameful passion!   To restore him after so
many falls, great, irresistible, grace must be
vouchsafed.   Can he, after displaying such
ingratitude, contempt, and perfidy, expect it
without the most frightful presumption?

" The very goodness of GOD increases thy
wickedness ; the abundance of His mercy en-
courages thee in sin."—*Tert.*

Temptation.

ART thou tempted? Be not discouraged.
GOD would try thy virtue first, then
crown it.   The Saint of saints was tempted.

His example must be thy consolation and strength. Art thou tempted? *Fly*, if thou canst: there is no disgrace in flight; it is not cowardice, but prudence and courage. Thanks be to GOD for having given the victory—not to courage and resistance—but to precaution and flight. All cannot fight, but who cannot fly? Weak and faint-hearted as we are, we should be often overcome did victory always depend on the way we fought; but however potent our foes may be they cannot prevail against him who has the wisdom to fly.

If thou canst not fly, *pray*. This is CHRIST's own command. The Apostles suffered the consequences of neglecting it when, instead of watching and praying, they slumbered in the garden of Olives. So unwatchful as to forsake prayer, they became so faint of heart as to forsake their Master. All our strength, under temptation, comes from GOD: it can only be obtained through prayer. We cannot have virtue without grace, nor grace without prayer.

If in spite of prayer the temptation continues, we must *fight*. However weak you be, however strong your foes, be not cast down. GOD is present in the conflict; offers help to sustain; holds out a crown to encourage; fights in you, with you, for you— what then have you to fear? As S. Paul exclaims, *If God be for us, who can be against us ?*[1] The victory is certain if we do our duty ; none are overcome save they who court defeat.   As long as we fight, we cannot be defeated ; as long as we are not defeated, the victory is ours ; and, with it, an immortal crown.

"Then art thou most in danger of defeat when thou seest not thy foes."—*S. Jerome.*

Covetousness a Snare.

THE immoderate love of pelf is con-demned by reason as well as faith. One need not be a Christian to comprehend the in-jurious results of this passion ; one need only use one's reason.   For what can be more foolish than an immoderate love of wealth, which cannot be eagerly desired without sin, or greedily grasped without wrong-doing ? A man's desires are never satisfied by riches, but only stimulated ; they do not make him a better man, but often a worse.

Faith condemns still more severely the im-moderate love of wealth.   How can a Chris-

[1] Rom. viii. 31.

tian suffer this passion to possess him when he reads the Gospel? Do not the maledictions launched by our LORD against the covetous come home to him? Does he not tremble when he hears Him protesting that *it is easier for a camel to go through the eye of a needle than for a rich man to enter into the kingdom of God?*[1] or announcing the unhappy fate of the rich man who seems to have been guilty of no other crime than that of loving his wealth too fondly instead of making a good use of it?[2] Surely a rich man ought to regard his state with humility and fear when he contrasts it with that of his LORD who was born and lived and died in poverty!

When a man eagerly seeks wealth, he is seeking obstacles to his salvation. To possess great wealth without clinging to it is difficult; to cling to it without falling into sin is impossible. The very reason which makes him seek wealth ought to make him dread it. He seeks it to gratify his desires and affections—and these are nearly always evil. To punish and destroy him, GOD has only to grant his wish.

" Thy kindness was the greater the less it suffered aught to grow sweet unto me that was not Thou."—*S. Aug.*

---

[1] S. Mark x. 25.   [2] S. Luke xvi. 19.

Almsgiving.

THE rich man in the Gospel was not an extortioner or unjust, but he was a hard man. This was his crime. We owe tribute to GOD in return for all our blessings; but as He needs nothing Himself, He transfers His rights to the poor. Mercy is the only sacrifice which GOD now demands at our hands; all others were abolished by the new Covenant. Alms are a debt which we owe to GOD; we rob Him when we fail to give them; we are His subjects, the poor His tax-gatherers, 'their hands His treasury.' The rich man is only a steward, who robs his Master when he feeds not His household.

We ought to practise almsgiving in order to discharge an obligation which Providence has as it were incurred. As the FATHER of all men, GOD provides for their maintenance. He might have done this Himself by an equal distribution of His gifts, but such an arrangement did not commend itself to His wisdom. Had there been an equality of wealth, men would have sought an equality of power. The result would have been a spirit of insubordination and anarchy. Hence it became necessary to provide a safe treasury for the poor, and what is it but the alms of the rich? If these then do not fulfil this obligation, the poor have nothing to rely upon, and are consequently encouraged to question the good providence of GOD. *Your abundance*, saith the Apostle, is *a supply for* the poor man's *want;*[1] your superfluities meet their necessities. That wasted wealth, saith S. Basil, that hoarded silver is not yours; if the beggar perishes for want of it, you are his murderer. His misery invokes vengeance upon your hard heart, and arms mercy itself against you. Alas! where shall be your refuge if even mercy condemns you?

Covetousness, vanity, and ambition have nothing, while charity has always much to bestow. Moderate then your desires, and you will find something to spare. Remember that as a Christian you are called upon to renounce the pomps and vanities of the world, and then you will find funds enough for the necessities of the poor. Many a family has been ruined by play and evil courses, not one so much as inconvenienced by almsgiving.

" Test thy faith; see whether thou canst

[1] 2 Cor. viii. 14.

lend unto the LORD, or whether thou canst trust thy slave but not thy Master."—*S. Aug.*

The Magdalene.

SINCE we cannot prevent, we must at least promptly follow the call of grace. Our own vileness and self-interest, as well as the honour of Him Who seeks us demand this. To put off for a single moment is often to risk all, to lose all. The foolish virgins came a minute too late and found that *the door was shut.*[1] The Magdalene was wiser. No sooner does she hear of JESUS than she seeks Him. Neither interests, nor loves, nor human respect, nor censorious remarks, nor ridicule, restrain her; she hears none of these things because she is listening to the call of grace.

What fervour she displays at her conversion! She sacrifices loves, pleasures, the world, everything to GOD. They are nothing to her now, for He is everything. Condemning her eyes, which have kindled impure fires in the hearts of men, to tears, she bathes her SAVIOUR's feet, and wiping them with her

---

[1] S. Matth. xxv. 10.

hair, turns the instruments of past vanity into instruments of repentance. Do you imitate her penitent fervour? do you follow the Apostle's advice, *Yield not ye your members as instruments of unrighteousness unto sin, ... but as instruments of righteousness unto God?*[1] Alas, how far you fall short of this! So weak a repentance as yours does not deserve the name, nay, it deserves itself to be repented of.

The LORD wished her to be wholly His, and as there had been no restraint exercised in satisfying her passions and inclinations, He desired that there should be none in her present endeavours to obey and please GOD. She did not disappoint Him, but proved the reality of her penitence by loving Him more than she had ever loved the world.

"Alas! the time when I loved Thee not, the days of grievous sin."—*S. Aug.*

Worldliness.

WE are not Christians unless we *have the Spirit of Christ;*[2] we have not the

---

[1] Rom. vi. 13.   [2] Rom. viii. 9.

Spirit of CHRIST unless we have renounced
the spirit of the world.   An infinite and insurmountable *enmity* exists between the spirit
of CHRIST and the spirit of the world.   Communion is as impossible between them as between light and darkness.[1]   Hence is it that
S. John exhorts Christians not to love the
world, and adds that *if any man love the world,
the love of the Father is not in him.*[2]   He that
gains the love of the one, must inevitably gain
the hatred of the other.

Far from praying for the *world,*[3] CHRIST
strikes it with a malediction.   How great
then is the blindness of Christians who justify
their conduct on the plea that it is the way of
the world!   That is the very reason why
they should act otherwise, for have they not
promised to renounce the world?   Think you
that, when standing before the Judgment-seat
of CHRIST, it will avail you aught to say that
all wherein you have displeased Him, was
done to please His bitterest enemy, the world?
will He not make that the ground of your
condemnation?

Now, it is easy to admit that the world is
the enemy of CHRIST,—to deny this would be
giving the lie to the Gospel,—but yet it is

[1] 2 Cor. vi. 14.   [3] 1 S. John ii. 15.
[2] S. John xvii. 9.

hard to admit frankly that one is, for all that, on the best of terms with the world. It is easy to endorse in a general way the condemnation of the world : how acquit what eternal Wisdom has condemned ? but it is difficult to condemn its particular maxims when they form the rule of one's conduct. What is the world ? It is an excessive love of wealth, pleasures, and honours. Have you this threefold love ? Then you are a worldling, and one of the subjects of the SAVIOUR's malediction : *Woe unto you that are rich ! . . . woe unto you that laugh now ! . . . . . woe unto you when all men shall speak well of you !*[1]

"Be one of the few, if thou wouldst hereafter be one of the saved."—*S. Aug.*

The Aims of Mortification.

THE first aim of Christian mortification is the ordering of our pleasures. We must have done with all sinful ones whatsoever. How find pleasure in that which robs GOD of glory, and renders us liable to eternal misery ? Then we must forbid ourselves, as

[1] S. Luke vi. 24—26.

a rule, dangerous ones.   For who would partake of a dish, however dainty, which had possibly been poisoned ?   Again, we must not allow our pleasures to become excessive or continuous.   For they are remedies vouchsafed by GOD to our infirmities, and would cease to be such if they became habitual. Again, we must sometimes abstain even from the most innocent pleasures, because, as S. Gregory says, having fallen into sin through indulgence in forbidden things, we must raise ourselves by abstaining even from things lawful.

The second aim of mortification is to govern a man's whole faculties and powers.   It curbs undue activity and curiosity of spirit ; regulates the heart's emotions,—its desires, affections, joys, fears, and aversions ; represses the licence and wanderings of the imagination ; arrests unruly and violent passions, and prevents their getting the mastery over the reason and will, or if they break loose brings them back under control, and punishes their excesses.   It restrains sallies of wit ; watches stirrings of self-love, and silences subtle whisperings of self-complacency.

The third aim of mortification is to teach us to submit to the cares and troubles, the occupations and responsibilities, and, in fine, all the duties of our position ; to bear willingly crosses whether caused by the injustice of our enemies, such as calumny and persecutions, or by the justice of GOD using His creatures to punish and try us, or by tedious and painful diseases. It teaches us to bear them in a penitential spirit, persuaded that our sufferings are less than we deserve ; to endure not with patience only but with gratitude, rejoicing in that the empire of the flesh is losing its hold over us, the body of sin being destroyed, the old man being crucified, and we ourselves nailed with JESUS CHRIST upon the Cross. This is what mortification comprises. Hast thou ever practised it ?

" Wouldst have the flesh obey thy spirit ? let thy spirit obey GOD ; let Him rule thee, and thou shalt rule thyself."—*S. Aug.*

Obedience.

THE virtue of obedience makes us carry out the commands of GOD and His representatives. It applies to all sorts and conditions of men. It is a universal duty binding upon all men because, in respect of one thing or another, there must always be some *that have the rule over them.*[1] Scripture declares that *to obey is better than sacrifice,*[2] because, as S. Gregory explains, in the one case the flesh of animals, in the other the will of man, is sacrificed. Sacrifices offered in a spirit of disobedience become abominable.

Our perfection consists in doing the will of GOD. I am certain that I do it when I obey my superior in anything that is not contrary to GOD's law. This is an article of faith: *He that heareth you, heareth Me; and he that despiseth you, despiseth Me.*[3] My superior may not always be reasonable in what he commands, but reason demands my obedience. Blind and irrational though obedience at times appear, it is always most enlightened and consistent with the highest reason—the will of GOD. My superior sins when his commands are dictated by passion, but my obedience is meritorious when it springs from charity. How blessed is the lot of the obedient! Assured of GOD's guidance, can they fear lest they be unwisely governed?

The practice of obedience in past ages was difficult, because man dearly loves liberty. The example of a GOD-man was necessary. Nothing is said of Him from His twelfth to

[1] Heb. xiii. 17.　　[2] 1 Sam. xv. 22.　　[3] S. Luke x. 16.

His thirtieth year save that *He was subject to His parents.*[1] Such is the summary of all the actions, all the virtues, all the marvels of His hidden life. "He was subject"—to whom? to His own creatures, to Joseph and Mary—in what? in the meanest and most laborious offices — how? promptly, readily, anticipating every wish, thoroughly, leaving nothing undone, perfectly, recognising in their will the will of His FATHER, and consequently obeying them as He would obey Him. Is it thus that you obey? Nay, your murmurings, the difficulties you raise, your perpetual remonstrances, your want of alacrity, your negligence, all show how far you fall short of the perfect obedience of JESUS Who declared that He had not come to seek His *own will, but the will of His Father,*[2] and Who, after practising obedience continually in life, desired to exhibit it in death, preferring, as saith S. Bernard, to cease to live than to cease to obey.[3]

"The foundation of all religion is obedience and fear."—*S. Cypr.*

[1] S. Luke ii. 51. [2] S. John v. 30.
[3] It is to be regretted that our author has not said more on a virtue so universally neglected both by Clergy and laity as obedience. The reader may consult Bp. Taylor's *Great Exemplar*, Sect. V., Disc. II., 18—26, and *Holy Living*, chap. III., Sect. I.

𝕿𝖍𝖊 𝕾𝖎𝖓𝖋𝖚𝖑𝖓𝖊𝖘𝖘 𝖔𝖋 𝖑𝖎𝖙𝖙𝖑𝖊 𝕾𝖎𝖓𝖘.

GOD is our FATHER ; our behaviour to-wards Him ought therefore to be that of children. Now, what sort of a son is he who confines his duty towards his father to obeying him in matters of importance, and to sparing him acts of gross disrespect, but who does not shrink from displeasing or annoying him on countless occasions, treating him without consideration or regard, and paying him none of those little attentions which are truer tests of tenderness than those essential duties the neglect of which would be quite unnatural ? Would a father have reason to feel satisfied with such conduct ? Would he not feel it more keenly than the disobedience or insolence of a servant ? And yet this is how we treat GOD. No wonder He feels such treatment more than the gross offences of libertines and unbelievers.

We do not value a friend who will only help us when we are in the greatest danger and last extremity. Heaven keep us from ever being so unfortunate as to need his aid ! We value one who is on the alert to seize every opportunity of pleasing us, and who is afraid of annoying us in the smallest matter.

Such a friend says to himself, 'Tis a trifle, but my friend would not like it; so I will leave it alone. Nothing is a trifle which pleases or displeases a friend. He who thinks otherwise does not know what friendship means. Alas, LORD, can I say that I love Thee when I am so ready to displease Thee by committing faults which I call little simply because I love Thee little?

Once more, imagine a bride priding herself on her faithfulness to her marriage vows, while acting with the utmost imprudence, and treating her husband with cold indifference while lavishing her tenderest attentions on a stranger! Now, JESUS is our Spouse, a jealous Spouse, loving tenderly those whom He regards as His own. Will He then patiently submit to be robbed of their affections, and see them given to His enemy, the world? will He be insensible to their faithlessness? Oft-repeated slights or proofs of inattention on the part of a friend are more painful than the hatred or violence of a foe. How much need, then, O LORD, have I to dread the many occasions, light though they seemed, on which I have treated Thee with indifference and disloyalty? how can I expect, after such conduct, those extraordinary graces which I yet so often need?

"When a man yields to self-seeking he falls from love."—*De Imit. Christi.*

Meekness.

THE meekness of a Christian is not the out-come of a poor timid spirit, of a happy temperament, of careful rearing, or of a kindly disposition. It is a virtue of passing excellence, the fruit of a patience which is proof against all wrongs and injuries; of a deep humility which, deeming itself worthy of the utmost contempt, never thinks it has suffered too much; and of a continual mortification of the passions which it subjects so completely to reason and grace as to restrain the earliest symptoms of rebellion. It is an outpouring of the unction of the Spirit, and sure token of the fulness of CHRIST'S indwelling. Only a Christian can have this virtue, and he that hath it not, hath not the Spirit of CHRIST.

Meekness produces two results. First, it moderates and regulates anger. It does not utterly banish anger, for it is often justifiable, as well as efficacious in curing the faults of others. But the too frequent or ready indulgence of wrath is forbidden; it must never be exhibited without good reason. A meek man allows anger to support but never to get the better of reason; he checks violent and harsh behaviour; he avoids bitter and out-rageous language; he may reproach, but not in offensive terms; all his wrath springs from charity and zeal, not from passion. The punishments imposed are ever lighter than the faults, so that the culprit, if he be not blind, feels that they are aimed at his faults and not at himself. Do you observe this measure when angry? Think you it a good way to correct a fault, to commit a greater through the indulgence of immoderate anger?

Secondly, meekness smothers all resent-ment and banishes from the heart not only hatred and vindictiveness, but even coldness and indifference towards the offender. Far from giving way to abusive language, a per-fectly meek man does not even utter re . proaches; he feels the injury done to God, and the loss entailed on the evil-doer more than his own wrong; not satisfied with par-doning the offence, he seeks pardon at God's hand for the offender; far from hating his enemies, he loves them sincerely, or ra-ther he has no enemies except himself and sin.

"Our King conquered the devil through meekness."—*S. Aug.*

The Duty of imitating Christ.

WHEN man was created in the image of GOD, he was led by a deeply-rooted sense of duty, as well as by a natural instinct, to copy and perfect, by his actions, that divine likeness which had only been drawn in outline at his creation. The perfection and happiness of rational beings depend on likeness to their Creator. Unhappily, says S. Bernard, all their sins and sorrows have arisen from their wish to imitate GOD, but not in the right way. The Angel, instead of wishing to imitate His goodness, tried to imitate His greatness by making himself His peer; and GOD, to punish his pride, cast him down into the abyss. Man, again, aspired to the universal knowledge of good and evil—a knowledge which belongs to GOD alone—and was, as a punishment, condemned to ignorance and error. Hence it came to pass that the eternal Word was made man, and lived in a state of humility and poverty, that man might not only be able to imitate Him without sin or danger, but find all his perfection and happiness in becoming like Him. This is one of the results of the Incarnation.

GOD was made man, saith S. Chrysostom, in order that man, by copying Him, might in a manner become divine. He bore *the image of the earthly*, that we might *bear the image of the heavenly ;*[1] He was incarnate that He might be our model as well as our SAVIOUR. SAVIOUR He cannot be unless He be our example. It was not merely from the demon and eternal punishment that we required deliverance, but from the bondage of sin, from the tyranny of our passions, from covetousness, from sensuality, from anger, from pride. Now He could only deliver us from them by leading us to practise the opposite virtues, poverty, mortification, meekness, humility; and His example alone can inspire us with the love of virtues so contrary to our natural instincts and inclinations. The necessity of practising, at least the great excellence of these virtues had never been realized by mankind before the Incarnation of our LORD. Since then, however, His example has so clearly demonstrated their value, and facilitated their practice, that we are left without excuse if we fail to imitate it. In every action of His

[1] 1 Cor. xv. 49.

life He tells us what He said when washing His disciples' feet : *I have given you an example, that ye should do what I have done to you.*[1]   He will never be our SAVIOUR unless He is now our model ; we shall never follow Him in His glory, unless we are following Him in His humiliation.

" To enter by the door is to enter by CHRIST, to enter by CHRIST is to imitate His life."—*S. Aug.*

True Contrition.

CONTRITION is of two kinds.   Used in a strict sense it implies generous disinterested pain and grief at having offended and displeased a GOD of infinite goodness. The second and less perfect kind is called attrition, a somewhat selfish remorse arising from the thought of our having subjected ourselves to His wrathful displeasure and the penalties of sin.   Neither the one nor the other can justify a sinner, or constitute true penitence, unless the sorrow produced exceeds

[1] S. John xiii. 15.

every other kind of sorrow. GOD is our sovereign Good; hence we must love Him above everything: sin is our sovereign evil; hence we must hate it above everything. Such a hatred can alone destroy and blot out sin, and constitute true penitence.

If you entertained a thorough hatred of sin, you would dread it more than poverty, disease, shame, or death itself. But your small dread of committing, or hatred of the sight of it; your ease of mind after its commission; your indifference or insensibility under the loss of your GOD; the little eagerness you exhibit in repairing so vast a loss; your lack of courage in overcoming obstacles to the attainment of this end,—all prove that you are very far from having a sovereign hatred of sin, and that you do not regard GOD as your sovereign Good, since you do not regard evil, which is infinitely opposed to Him, as your sovereign evil. How then can you flatter yourself that you are truly penitent? What is your penitence but a delusion and a snare?

" Hatred of sin alone creates true penitence."—*S. Aug.*

Repentance delayed.

WHY put off your conversion to a future time? Are you sure of the future? GOD alone can insure you it. Has He guaranteed it? has He not threatened the very contrary? The present alone is yours: why not turn it to account? time is short, it passes swiftly by: why waste it? You say, I will change by-and-by: but why not now? How long will you go on repeating the words used by Augustine when he was resisting grace, " Soon, soon, shortly, shortly ; but ' soon' was late, and ' shortly' was long in coming?" why not rather say with the same Augustine, now determined to obey the call of grace, " How long shall it be to-morrow, to-morrow? why not to-day? why not this moment?"

You need grace to repent; it is offered now and you reject it. Do not your contempt and neglect render you unworthy of it? The longer you put off your conversion, the more your sins will be multiplied, and GOD alienated. What can you hope from the anger of GOD? After living so long in sin you will need extraordinary grace for your conversion: such a measure of grace is a token of special favour: can you expect it from One Whom you have treated with such insolence and contempt? On what then do you rest your hopes of ultimate conversion? Is yours not a blind presumption?

Repentance requires a will strong and sincere enough to carry it out. The longer you delay, the weaker your will becomes; your sins multiply, your passions gain strength, bad habits get confirmed, your reason ceases to restrain, and your understanding darkens. Will all this render your conversion an easier task hereafter? will the obstacles not prove almost insurmountable? you cannot break with sin when it is holding you by a thread— how will you when fastened to it with a rope? Is it not evident, that if you delay your conversion you run the risk of never being converted at all, and of dying impenitent?

" When thou readest that thou shalt have mercy on repentance, tell me if it is written how long thou hast to live."—*S. Aug.*

Degrees of Humility.

BY humility we acquire such a thorough knowledge of ourselves, that self-esteem

o

and the love of men's praise are effectually shut out. There are several degrees of this virtue. The first consists not only in acknowledging on our knees before GOD that we are nothing—that we have nothing which we can claim, unless it be sin and sorrow, and that we can do nothing save ruin and slay our souls—but also in feeling content that it should be so, in despising ourselves from the bottom of our hearts, in taking credit for nothing that we have done, in shrinking from praise because our hearts tell us it is undeserved, and in walking before GOD with confusion of face, rejoicing that the good that may be in us is not our own but His.

The second degree of humility consists in submitting patiently to contempt. If we regard it as a real evil, we must bear it for GOD's sake ; if, as often happens, it is but an imaginary evil, we must not trouble ourselves about it. Either it is deserved, or it is not. If it is, what right have we to complain ? if it is not, they who despise us hurt themselves far more than they do us. Men of the world are wont to say, Return contempt for contempt ; but a Christian not only submits to it, but pities and frames excuses for his revilers. Secure of GOD's approval, he cares little for the world's.

The highest degree of humility reaches the point of even loving contempt. A real blessing ought always to be desired. And is it not a blessing when viewed by the light of faith, since it enables us to sacrifice to CHRIST that which is dearest to us—our honour; since it renders us the objects of GOD's good pleasure and love, Who cannot but be pleased with so costly a sacrifice; since it is a method of becoming like unto GOD Who was despised and emptied of His glory? Nothing should humble us more than our excessive dread of humiliation, for faith teaches us in what light our LORD regarded, and how readily He embraced it.

"In vain seekest thou the virtue of humility while avoiding the path of humiliation."—*S. Bern.*

Crucified to the World.

TO know the world is to despise it—so blind in its judgments, so unjust in its esteem and rewards. It regards neither virtue nor merit, and unworthiness is often a title to its praise. It is untrue to its promises, inconsistent in its ways, inconstant in its friendship. Its favour is dearly purchased, hardly preserved, quickly lost. It is a weak friend, a dangerous foe; its promises deceive, its flatteries destroy.

But it is not enough to despise, we must be weaned from the world. How many appear to scorn, who yet cling to it! Its vanity is their perpetual theme, and yet they love it; its faithlessness is a daily complaint, and yet they trust it; the constant object of their imprecations, no idol has more worshippers!

They who aspire after Christian perfection must not only be weaned from, but dead to the world. *Ye are dead*, saith S. Paul, *and your life is hid with Christ in God.*[1] Men may be weaned from, without being insensible to the world's good things; without seeking, perhaps they find their happiness in them. But a dead man is insensible to everything. Splendid obsequies, magnificent mausoleums, the loud trumpetings of universal praise, are nothing now to him; they touch him not. Such is the picture of one dead to the world; such is the portrait of S. Francis Borgia. Though he met with the most splendid successes—though his virtues, his heroic actions, the marvels he performed, drew upon him the

[1] Col. iii. 3.

applause and esteem and veneration of the greatest men—he felt them no more than if they had not concerned him. He was dead to the world and to self. Insensible to all besides, he was sensitive only where GOD's glory was at stake. Happy deadness which makes a soul live to GOD! Alas! is my lively concern for my happiness and worldly interests not a proof that I am far from this blessed state?

" The soul is more where it loveth than where it liveth."[1]—*S. Aug.*

Sloth.

SLOTH is the parent of many other sins. Nearly all sins of omission are its offspring. It is accompanied with a distaste for religion and great negligence in ascertaining and following the path of duty, owing to a want of courage to surmount difficulties. A very common sin, it is little known. People are willing to remain ignorant of their obligations,-because they are unwilling to discharge

---

[1] Dr. Pusey's rendering of " Anima magis est ubi amat, quam ubi animat."

them; or if ignorance cannot be pleaded as an excuse for their neglect, a thousand reasons, such as delicate health, the difficulty or impossibility of fulfilling them, are put forward. The unprofitable servant in the Gospel excused his conduct on the plea that his master was a *hard man*.[1] He himself it should seem was wholly blameless, the fault lay entirely with his master! How many bury their talents, and hide them even from themselves, to be saved the trouble of turning them to account!

The slothful often mistake for virtues the simple results of a sluggish temperament. Thus they take for humility and modesty the contempt they show for lofty positions and the calls of ambition, when it simply proceeds from their dread of the trouble which would be entailed upon them. So again they take for temperance the little eagerness they feel in the pursuit of pleasure, while, at bottom, this arises from the trouble it would cost them to purchase pleasure, and from their considering indolence and idleness the highest pleasure. Theirs is not a spirit of unworldliness, but a simple love of ease. They that would be saved must overcome their passions, surmount great obstacles, and discharge difficult duties. How are the slothful to do this?

[1] S. Matth. xxv. 24.

"Be not slothful, be not listless: eternal life is thy reward."—*S. Aug.*

ꜰrequent Self-Examination.

NOTHING is more useful than a nightly examination of the conscience. It is the most effectual means of acquiring that perfect self-knowledge which is as rare as it is needful. It should be our rule at set times to retire into ourselves for the purpose of discovering and remedying our infirmities. Nothing tends more to keep men in a humble frame than a frequent review of their conduct —they are self-satisfied simply because they rarely think about it. The most useful result of frequent introspection is the undoing of bad habits. They have been contracted by oft-repeated acts of sin: they can only be eradicated by as frequent a use of the contrary acts—and it is these that self-examination should be the means of exercising. Even the heathen have recognised the great benefit of self-knowledge.

But superficial self-examination is not enough. It must be thorough. We must not content ourselves with a hurried review of the day: this will only deceive us. We must retire into ourselves and diligently search our ways. After frequent examinations how few really know what is lying at the bottom of their hearts! Is it not because we content ourselves with seeking out grave sins, and leaving others unnoticed, which, if less grievous, are not less dangerous in their results? Do we not lightly pass over many a sin of omission, many a neglect of grace, many a sinful drawing of our deceitful desires, many an occasion on which vanity, love of men's praise, or self-interest, has sullied our best actions and deprived us of their reward?

Let us strive most earnestly to conceive a lively sorrow for our sins, and form a firm, effectual resolution to amend. We must not content ourselves with a general resolution to abandon our sins, but attack that sin which holds us fastest, and leave nothing undone to free ourselves from its grasp. No fault must be suffered to go unpunished: let each have its appropriate penalty.

"Busy with our neighbour's faults, blind to our own."—*S. Chrys.*

Meditation.

HOW little faith there is among Christians! It is not indeed totally absent; the verities of religion and maxims of the Gospel are not deliberately questioned, but they are taken for granted; they are not received with lively faith, or fathomed, or searched out. And what is more calculated to make ours a living energising faith than the practice of serious reflection in our devotions? Surely the paramount importance of divine truths must, when duly realised, make a deep impression on our hearts and minds, and force us to put our hands to the work of thoroughly reforming our lives. And is it not meditation that enables us to penetrate and taste these truths? So that it may be said that just as want of faith is the cause of most sins, so want of meditation on the great maxims of the Gospel is the cause of our want of faith. Most men live without rule because they live without meditation.

It is impossible to succeed in an important transaction, which is not only arduous in itself, but thwarted by powerful enemies full of vigilance and stratagems, unless the means of overcoming their opposition, and defeating their measures are carefully sought. The devil, knowing how important meditation is to our salvation, never fails to suggest many empty pretexts to deter us from its practice.

Some plead the engrossing nature of their business which leaves them no time. But can there be a more important business than that of our salvation? And if meditation be a necessary condition of securing it, can the busiest plead any excuse for neglecting this duty? Others, again, plead mental distraction rendering it impossible to fix their thoughts on any subject. But does it prevent their reflecting, in any matter of importance, upon the means which may be successfully employed, and upon the obstacles which may stand in their way? And why can they not do as much when their salvation is at stake? They are not called upon to task their powers of reflection beyond this point.

" Prayer without meditation is but tepid."
—*S. Aug.*

Too late!

YOU admit that repentance is necessary; the Gospel teaches you that there is no salvation for a sinner without repentance, and you know that you are one. But you want to put it off till you are going to die. Why this delay? Men cannot do too soon what, left undone, deprives them of eternal life. Who has promised you time to repent at death? has GOD not threatened the contrary? How many die suddenly every day who have clung to the same expectation! Ah! remember, saith S. Chrysostom, that your soul, your salvation, is at stake. You make a matter of such importance depend upon a chance while you take so many precautions in the case of trifles.

But, assuming that you will have sufficient time, and that your death will not be sudden, will you in your last hours be in a condition to give your thoughts to repentance? Are you sure that your mind will be sufficiently free and disengaged to apply itself to so difficult a work? Shall a man whose frame is oppressed by the violence of disease, over whose senses a deadly lethargy has crept, whose powers are paralyzed, whose mind is prostrated ; who is overpowered at the thought of leaving all he has loved best, distracted at the sight of a thousand frightful spectres, in horrible suspense about his eternal future, and unable to apply himself to the most trifling matters,—shall such a man be able to give himself to so important a business as a searching self-examination and confession of the sins of his life, to feel a lively sorrow for the past, and form steadfast resolutions for the future ?

But, granting that your mind will be unclouded, will your heart be so entirely detached and weaned from sin as true repentance requires ? If so, you must forsake sin beforehand, and not wait till it forsakes you. A true penitent sovereignly loves all that he has sovereignly hated, that is to say, GOD, his soul, and eternal things ; he sovereignly hates all that he has sovereignly loved, sin, the world, and the flesh. The covetous man must become liberal, the sensual chaste, the proud humble, the passionate gentle. Can all this be done in a moment? Can evil habits be changed as quickly as a garment ? Not without a miracle of grace ; and who dares without frightful presumption, rest the hopes of his salvation upon a miracle ? Scripture mentions the conversion of only one thief. It was a miracle wrought in the presence of a dying GOD!

" The means of conversion must never be put aside, lest the opportunity of correction be lost for ever."—*S. Aug.*

Idleness.

MAN was not suffered to be idle even in a state of innocence. He enjoyed rest, but not such rest as excluded action. His work did not fatigue him; it was an occupation, not a toil. But when he fell, GOD condemned him to painful labour, saying unto him, *In the sweat of thy face shalt thou eat bread.*[1] No sooner had Adam sinned than he was made to toil. Alas! the greatest sinners are the idlest men because they are impenitent. Real repentance would make them active, and cause them to bring forth its fruits; but in a spirit of rebellion they try to escape the sentence pronounced upon them in the person of Adam.

We must avoid idleness if we would avoid

---

[1] Gen. iii. 19.

P

mischief. It is the mother and teacher of all sin. He who has nothing to do is capable of doing anything. The busy man has only one temptation to fear, the idle lies open to all,—the demon can attack him at a thousand points. The best remedy for temptation, especially that of impurity, is occupation. What is the cause of the evil courses of many young persons? It is idleness. Give them something to do, and they will keep upright.

Idleness must be avoided if we would get through all our duties. They who know their number and importance only complain of want of time. They who have any to spare, are either ignorant of their responsibilities or wilfully neglect them. How many obligations devolve on Christians if they only care to fulfil them ! Who can pretend to have nothing to do while there remain so many mourners to comfort, so much poverty, sickness, and shame to assist, so many in prison to visit ? CHRIST's poor members left destitute, His altars left bare, call on thee to work and help, —and thou hast nothing to do !

"Always be doing something, that the devil may always find thee busy!"—*S. Jerome.*

Temptation.

THE HOLY SPIRIT warns us that we must prepare for temptation as soon as we resolve to give ourselves to GOD's service. Nothing sometimes is more to be feared than freedom from temptation. It is often a sign either that GOD abandons us, or that the demon looks upon us as his own: there is no combat because we have ceased to resist. The greatest saints have been tempted: had they not, they would not have been great saints. CHRIST Himself, the Saint of saints, was tempted. Being our Head, it was His will to share our weakness that we might share His strength; being our Pattern, it was His will to teach us how to meet temptation; and, being our Redeemer, it was His will to merit, by submitting to the humiliation of temptation, grace sufficient to uphold us. So long as the flesh warreth against the Spirit, we shall have to fight. Alas! LORD, I carry my greatest foe in my own breast; unless Thou fightest in me I am lost.

Temptation is frequently a trial sent by GOD for our welfare. He permits it in order to test and bring out our virtues; *if thou come to serve the Lord, prepare thy soul for tempta-*

tion.[1] He permits it that we may feel our weakness and throw aside all self-trust, and that this experience of our incapacity of resisting our potent enemies may lay upon us the happy necessity of flying to Him Who alone makes all our strength. He permits it for our purification; for as fire tries and purifies gold, so does temptation purify the just man more and more.[2] By it virtues are acquired and exercised; by it the heavenly crown is won; by it we are kept out of that careless security which results from too protracted a state of peace.

To combat temptation with success we must, after the Apostle's advice, *give no place*[3] to it; persuade ourselves that it comes from the demon as soon as it is felt; never parley, but start back from it as though we had touched fire unawares. When the temptation is one of impurity, we must not allow the mind to dwell on it under the pretext of ascertaining whether we entertained the thought willingly. We must exercise the greatest vigilance, realize the all-seeing eye of GOD, dwell on the Passion of JESUS CHRIST, pray unceasingly—an indispensable duty in the moment of temptation—and, lastly, never losing

[1] Ecclus. ii. 1.   [2] Job xxiii. 10.
[3] Eph. iv. 27.

heart when we fall, rise again with confusion of face, and yet with confidence.

" Strength is imparted from above not to make us presumptuous, but cautious."—*S. Cypr.*

The single Eye.

THE first defect that creeps into our best actions is a slight admixture of self-seeking. Our only object should be to please and seek GOD in all our acts, but unless we are constantly on the watch over our hearts, we shall find it impossible to forget and lose sight of ourselves. Self-love deceives us so cleverly that, often, when we flatter ourselves that we have turned it out, it gets in again by a back door, and is nearest when supposed to be farthest off. To guard against this, let us frequently ask ourselves this question,—Am I seeking GOD alone in what I am doing? The answer may probably be given in the affirmative when we are equally ready for things good and evil, smooth and hard, sweet and bitter, and when humiliation and mortification are deliberately chosen as often as we believe that we shall thus please GOD best.

A second defect is to act on the spur of the moment, through caprice, or from a simple love of activity. The best actions, so performed, become imperfect. A Christian must act under the motions of grace, otherwise he often does a thing at the wrong time, and with undue haste. Caprice is taken for love, impetuosity for zeal. Now to remedy this we must curb our natural eagerness, and as far as possible not take any matter, however praiseworthy, in hand until we feel ourselves to be in a calmer frame of mind.

The third defect is the pain we feel as often as we fail in what we have taken in hand,—a trouble caused by self-love and conceit. We hoped to succeed and gain credit; we have failed, and so we feel mortified and humiliated. Had we solely sought GOD's glory and the accomplishment of His will, we had been at peace; for He is glorified when we are humiliated, and His will is none the less accomplished when our plans miscarry. Besides, it is better to be humbled by failure than puffed up by success; and if we miss our object, we at least earn the reward of humility and of a single intention which is all that GOD expects at our hands.

"Seek JESUS in all things, and thou shalt

at least find Him : seek self, and thou shalt find it to thy cost."—*De imit. Christi.*

The one Thing needful.

HAPPY soul which, stripped and weaned from everything, desires and seeks GOD alone, and abandons itself entirely to Him! It is such a soul that S. Paul describes as *having nothing, yet possessing all things;*[1] it has chosen *that good part* which the Magdalene chose, and which could *not be taken from* her.[2] Such a soul cries out to GOD in a holy transport, I reckon it wealth indeed to be stripped and weaned from all the good things of earth, too rich if only I possess my GOD. I esteem it true happiness to be deprived of all the pleasures of the flesh and the world provided I enjoy communion with GOD. I hold it to be the highest glory to renounce all personal glory and honour, if only I can, by self-humiliation, increase the glory of GOD.

A man thus emptied of self has no will but GOD's, no desire, no hope, no stay but GOD. He would belong to GOD only and find everything in Him. With S. Francis, he exclaims,

---

[1] 2 Cor. vi. 10.   [2] S. Luke x. 42.

My GOD and my all. What does he care for anything else? To whom GOD is everything, the world is nothing. He thoroughly realises the frame of mind of David when he exclaimed, *Whom have I in Heaven but Thee? and there is none upon earth that I desire in comparison of Thee.*[1] Such are the feelings of a detached soul. You do not understand them because you do not love. Give me, saith S. Augustine, a GOD-loving soul, and it will comprehend, because it feels what I say; to an unloving soul I speak in an unknown tongue.

What happiness does a soul find in self-abandonment to the guidance of GOD! Such a soul is more closely united to GOD than it is to the body in which it dwells. It can repose on His breast like a babe on the breast of its mother; it can lie there tranquilly and take its rest in peace.[2]

"Having Thee, what more do we want?" —*S. Aug.*

---

[1] Ps. lxxiii. 24.

[2] Such language *ought* to represent the feelings of mature Christians, for it implies no higher standard than the Gospel's, but how few can use it!

Excuses of Non-Communicants.

IT is strange that instead of seeking reasons for coming often to the Communion, seeing how great a benefit it is, we should seek reasons for absenting ourselves. One says, I am unworthy. Are you then waiting till you are worthy? If so you will never come. What saint ever felt himself worthy? We are in a good frame of mind for communicating when we think ourselves unworthy and do all in our power to come in a worthy spirit. Humility supplements our lack of merit. If you renounce sin with sincere grief and a steadfast resolution never to commit it again, you are worthy. Otherwise we should be making that a condition of communicating which is its fruit. When the SAVIOUR administered the Communion to His disciples, were they already perfect? Far from it.

Another says, I am so cold, so listless, so feeble. What! you will not come to the fire because you are cold? nor take nourishment because you are feeble? nor medicine because you are sick? What folly! If you are cold can you do better than approach this furnace of divine love? if feeble, strengthen yourself by eating the bread of the strong; if sick, take the efficacious and universal remedy for all the ills of the soul. Others complain of the small profit they derive. But whose fault is that? As a matter of fact, which make the greater progress in virtue—frequent or rare communicants? Perhaps GOD is hiding your progress from yourself to keep you humble. If your evil desires are less violent, if your passions are less strong, if you show greater courage in resisting temptation, if you fall into sin less frequently and grievously—is this not a result of your communions?

Although frequent are more desirable than rare communions, it is a notion opposed to reason, to the sentiments of the Fathers, and the practice of the most experienced spiritual guides, to suppose that it is advisable or possible for all Christians to communicate daily, as some maintain.

"If it is thy *daily* bread, why take it *yearly?*"—*S. Amb.*

Sufferings improved.

IT is not a misfortune to suffer, since JESUS CHRIST says, *Blessed are they that mourn,* but it is a great misfortune to make a bad use of suffering. Sufferings are that Gospel treasure which few men find, or rather which all men find but which few turn to account, because they know not its value. We find in the Cross, saith a holy man, salvation, life, protection of GOD, abundance of spiritual consolations, strength of soul, joy of spirit, the epitome of all virtues, and the perfection of holiness. What wealth !

And yet what Christian does not misuse it? The Cross is our life and salvation, and, through our own fault, we find in it death and ruin; it should be a source of consolation, and it becomes an occasion of discontent and murmuring; it should make our joy and our strength, and it plunges us into despair; it is the sure means of acquiring holiness, and we render it a subject of sin; it is the shortest path to Heaven, and we make it a way to hell !

To turn sufferings to good account we must bear them patiently. Otherwise our crosses will prove worse than useless. If we bear our cross patiently it will bear us, or cease to be a cross; but if unwillingly, if we drag it along, it will overpower us. To suffer in spite of oneself is to have a foretaste of hell; to share the fate of the impenitent thief who descended by the cross into hell, while the penitent mounted thereby into Heaven. GOD knows how much we are able to bear, and proportions our sufferings to our sins and to our strength.

"Wherein is the mercy of GOD not conspicuous, if even tribulation be a benefit?"— *S. Aug.*

Recollectedness.

NOTHING is more necessary to advancement in holiness than recollectedness. The difficulties pleaded as an excuse for neglecting it show how needful it is. The more a man is scattered abroad, the more he has need to retire from time to time into himself; the best employments otherwise tend to dissipation of mind. Things painful or pleasant, which present themselves in the way of our business, by arousing the passions, cause great distraction unless we be careful to return now and then into ourselves. The multitude of imperfect motives too, which mingle with our actions when we are off our guard, divide the heart. The greatest saints have bewailed this tendency to distraction which they have recognised in themselves. S. Bernard, after reproaching a great pope with this fault, deplored his having himself fallen into it. But we do not lament it because our very dissipation prevents our feeling its effects or dreading its results.

The heart of man cannot exist without some attachment. To live is to love, and to love is to be attached. He must be attached either to GOD or to the creature. If he has not a spirit of recollectedness, which consists principally in having GOD in his thoughts, he will not accustom himself to look for Him in His creatures, or raise his thoughts from them and fasten his affections on their Creator. Thus a man who seems zealous in all good works, and to be labouring with the single aim of detaching others from the world and the creature, shall find himself insensibly attached to them, owing to the neglect of recollectedness and vigilance.

"Remember at times to give thyself back to thyself."—*S. Bern.*

Habitual Sin.

TO commit a sin is a grave misfortune, but to commit it habitually is a still graver. It is easy to disentangle oneself from unaccustomed sin; it displeases even a corrupted heart in a thousand ways. But how rarely is an habitual sinner converted! It is a kind of miracle in the order of grace, of which the resurrection of Lazarus, after he had lain several days in the grave and had begun to stink, is a figure. Habit, saith S. Bernard, is a second nature; one changes in every other respect, but one does not part with one's nature and the habit of sin. Nearly all men act in accordance with their natural tendencies and habitual proclivities. Sin is readily committed, and iniquity swallowed like water.

S. Augustine calls a bad habit a slave under the empire of sin and the demon. Hard and cruel masters! I groaned, saith he, under the degrading bondage of my bad habit. My enemy had made a chain of my oft-repeated sins, linked together as it were, by which he held my will shamefully enthralled. I struggled ever and anon to regain my liberty, but habit held me tight; and I feared like death to see the course of my sinful ways arrested, which were causing me to die daily. Sin, which had turned into a habit, had more power over me than the good towards which I felt myself drawn; and the nearer the moment of my conversion drew, the deeper my dread became.

Habit imposes a kind of necessity of sinning. Great is the misfortune of having the power of sinning; greater still, of using that fatal power; but greatest of all, of being unable to refrain from sin—and this is the result of a bad habit. From an unlawful lust, saith S. Augustine, we pass on to a sinful action; the action oft repeated strengthens the lust; the lust strengthened changes into a habit; and the habit becomes a fatal necessity. And yet it is not a necessity which can be pleaded as an excuse, since it is not absolute, but arises from the wilful way in which we have abused our liberty by a voluntary self-abandonment to all kinds of sin. Unhappy necessity which increases our sins without palliating our guilt—which we might have resisted in time but can no longer escape!

"It must needs be an eternal torment to be eternally reminded of past sins."—*S. Aug.*